Confessions of the Hairstylist

7 Top Hair Industry Secrets Revealed

Anastasia Kravtsova

ISBN: 978-1-77277-076-6

PUBLISHED BY:
10-10-10 PUBLISHING
MARKHAM, ON
CANADA

Contents

To my sister, Antonina.
Inspirational woman, loving sister, caring mother, great wife
and an awesome daughter.
Love you.

Acknowledgements

I am taking "thank you" very seriously. Nowadays, "thank you" is overused. I say "thank you" when I mean it.

I would like to give a big thank you to the people who supported me, who believed in me and who helped make this book happen.

My Mom and Dad, for your unconditional love and support.
To my grandmothers, Galina and Elena.
To my brother-in-law, Dmytro Koval.
To my Aunt Lana and her family - Anatoly, Vitaly and Anna.
To my best friends - Charles M. and Wayne Smith.
To Pam Bjarak Mady and Carrie Mady.
To my salon landlord, John Bjarnason.
To my inspirational coaches, Raymond Aaron and Karyn Mullen.
To my teachers, Mr. Hopkinson, Margaret Muir, Mr. C., Ms. Zak and Ms. McCan.
To Sergey Andryanov.
To my awesome staff and coworkers - Tiia Kumpulainen, Lori Lawrence and Mila, for their dedication, work and support.

Huge thank you to my clients. Without you, I could not be who I am now.

"A smart-looking face is not a sign of intellect. All the dumb things in the world are done with that facial expression. Smile, gentlemen, smile."
Rudolf Erich Raspe "The Surprising Adventures of Baron Munchausen"

Foreword

Confessions of the Hairstylist is filled with important information, interesting stories, funny situations and inspirational lessons from Anastasia Kravtsova. She has spent years hairstyling people like you to be your most beautiful self. This book is ironic, funny, sassy, and helpful for stylists, hair salon clients, and women in general.

Confessions of the Hairstylist will reveal truths about the salon industry that you would have never heard before. Through stories and affirmations of clients, co-workers, and competitor salons, Anastasia shares her journey as a hairstylist, and as an immigrant. She immigrated to Canada 9 years ago and has been able to achieve huge success in her industry. Her story is now revealed to you through these very pages.

Take inspiration from Anastasia's story - she shares her journey, experiences, and the skills she has gained with you so that you can apply them to your own life. She feels that if a woman who immigrated to Canada could find success in this country, you can too. Nothing is impossible.

Her dedication, love for her work and great sense of humour are the secret to her success. By reading *Confessions of the Hairstylist,* you will get an inside look on Anastasia's journey to the successful woman she is today, and take inspiration on how you too can achieve greatness.

Raymond Aaron

New York Times Bestselling Author

Chapter 1
Fashion Is My Profession

"But I don't want to go among mad people," Alice remarked.
"Oh, you can't help that," said the Cat: "We're all mad here. I'm
mad. You're mad."
"How do you know I'm mad?" said Alice.
"You must be," said the Cat, "or you wouldn't have come here."
Lewis Carroll, Alice in Wonderland

Confession #1

Right after hairdressing school, I was working at a downtown salon.
There was a good looking man who came in every 2 weeks to fix his
haircut. He worked in the financial industry and had the look of a Wall
Street guy, typical white collar. That day, it just so happened that all
the senior hairstylists were busy and I was chosen to provide a service
for him. During the haircut, he was staring straight at my boobs. He
did not say a word. His eyes were following my curves. Even when I
was working on the back of his head, I saw him look into the reflection
of the mirror, focused right on my cleavage. Then I noticed the strange,
but frequent, repetitive movements of his hand under the cape. I could
not believe my eyes. Making the sound of a wounded bear, it was at

that moment when I realized - I am not going to do men anymore. I mean men's haircuts. Period!

Being a woman is not easy. Even though we are living in the 21st century and have the same rights as men, it is still a male dominated world. As near as 60 years ago, it was dramatically different for women. We try to be equal with men, act like men, compete with men and we are pretty successful at that. Nowadays, we (women) are raising kids and making money, we decide what we want, have a right to vote in elections, are running businesses and taking posts in politics, but we are still women. We also have a need to look pretty, feel capricious sometimes and be pampered. Sometimes we lack that masculine confidence and we compensate for it with a new hair style, a new dress or a new pair of shoes. I am a woman myself, so I know what I am talking about. That's why I decided to work exclusively with women, because I understand us.

For your information, in all my stories the names and identifying details have been changed to protect the privacy of the individuals. Thanks for understanding.

Confession #2

I had this blonde girl walk into my salon. She was tall, fit, gorgeous and looked like a model. Let's call her Mary. She requested highlights and colour to fix her roots. This type of service requires a couple of hours, so during the process, we talked. Usually people talk about what things are bothering them the most. Mary was 38 years old with a great job, not married and a child-free woman. She told me that currently she is single, but not 100%, as her relationship with her ex had been on and off for the last 7 years. As I understand it, she was still in love with her ex and could not move on. I think it's unhealthy, but I am here only to tell the story, not to judge.

When I finished my work, I showed her the final result – a beautiful rich blonde colour with dimension and depth as she requested. She looked at herself in the mirror. I expected any reaction, but not the one I got. She covered her face with her hands and started crying. I was confused. The colour had turned out beautifully. I didn't understand what was going on. She told me, "I can't look at myself. I look ugly."

"Well, don't you like the colour or maybe the blow out? What can I do for you or what do you want me to fix?"

"I don't know. It looks good, but I don't like it. I feel ugly and disgusting," she said as she was crying. "What can you do to make me look beautiful?"

I understood it was a psychological problem. Then she started talking again.

"I look so ugly. No wonder he cheats on me and doesn't love me. How can someone fall in love with a person like me. Look at that enormous

nose, thin lips, and huge forehead... Why am I so unlucky to be born so ugly?"

Apparently, she was depending on her ex. It is called mental abuse. Some men are so insecure that to improve their self-esteem, they act like control freaks – they destroy a woman and make her completely dependent on them. Her ex was a player. He broke up with her, but did not leave her alone. He was not living with her, but still had some clothes and belongings at her place and would come to pick up something at his convenience. Her confidence was crushed, she was not a happy person, suffering from low self-esteem, a victim of her own emotions. She had no strength to get out of that emotional dead end.

Mary needed a psychologist. This problem cannot be resolved by fixing her hair colour. But what can I do? Based upon my professional ethics, I can't say it. I felt bad for her, even though it was not my fault. I was upset all day. I felt sorry for a strange woman with whom I had only known for a couple of hours as I did her highlights, but also was mad at myself that I allowed those emotions to affect me. I am not perfect. I am a human being with my own weaknesses as well.

As you can see, sometimes it's not all about the look. With time, you become a kind of psychologist. Sometimes the problem is much deeper than just their outside. In the beauty industry, you need to have the ability to listen and to understand people, as well as be gentle enough not to hurt them even more.

This book is a mix of professional confessions and stories from my personal life to make you understand what kind of a person I am, where my experience comes from and make you realize that being a hairstylist is not an easy profession. We do it because we love it, and we deserve some respect. We all make our mistakes and we grow through it. We learn the lessons in our own way. I am not ashamed to admit my faults, because they are what make me grow and there are things that make me stronger even if it is a painful lesson.

Confession #3

I was married before. I was 20. He was 26. We met in Kyiv, Ukraine, where I am from and lived at that time. It was love at first sight. It was that pure, delicate feeling that came for the first time in my life for a man. Yes, he was my first love. Tall, good looking guy, a professional sportsman with big muscles and nice dark hair. Those alluring bottomless dark eyes just drove me crazy. When he hugged me, I felt so safe and so good. You know the feeling when thousands of butterflies are tickling in your stomach.

We were young, happy and in love.

After 6 months of dating, he proposed to me. I was the happiest girl in the world. Of course, I said, "Yes!" That summer we had a wedding like every girl dreams about when they are little - with a beautiful white dress and veil, guests, music, wine and the finest food. I felt like a princess that day. He was so serious and handsome. I had a feeling that nothing could destroy our happiness, as together we could move mountains.

Everything changed right after the wedding. He thought that now I belonged to him. I couldn't escape, as I was now married, so there was no need to be nice and gentle anymore. He started a new business and not everything was going smoothly. I tried to support him as much as I could. I was working as well, but I always tried to look good for him, cooking his favourite dishes and creating a calm and relaxing atmosphere at home, so he could relax and feel comfortable. I understood that my man was fighting to provide a living for us, so I did my best to be a good wife to him.

However, the business was not going well at all. Instead of quitting or changing it, he was putting himself into a deeper hole, causing him to suffer from stress and depression. As a result, he merged me into the negativity. He became very impatient, rude, and mentally abusive. Now I understand that he tried to take control of the situation the way he thought was right, but my dreams and love for him were broken.

We were too young to face the brutal reality of these financial and emotional hardships. Then it got worse. He found a new way to relax - marijuana. He used to say, "I am not drinking alcohol because of sports, so a couple puffs of weed will help me to relax and calm my mind."

Within the next half a year, it went from a couple puffs on the weekends to a couple of joints a day. Every day. He became addicted to marijuana and when it was not enough, he would smoke crack.

If you have never lived with a drug addicted person - you would not understand what kind of nightmare it is. He stopped working, and became a very aggressive and paranoid person. He refused to go and get help. We were living on my salary and, needless to say, almost all the money would go to drug dealers. He would scream at me and ask why I made so little money. He would say that I was stupid and just not able to make more. He was constantly repeating that he did me a huge favour by marrying me, as no other guy in the world would do it with such a stupid, ugly and miserable girl like me. He was cheating on me and not even hiding that. He would compare other girls to me, and of course, there was always someone who was better than me. He became a tyrant. When he made an offer to have me change my job and become a prostitute in order to make more money - that was the last straw. I understood that I needed to escape from this relationship or he would destroy my personality, my mind and my life completely. It should stop now, so I quickly packed my things and left to nowhere.

It was a tough and very painful chapter of my life. But at the same time, I did not become a hateful person and did not develop a victim complex. Believe it or not, I became kinder. I learned the hard way that everyone is fighting their own demons and you never know what's going on in a person's life behind those closed doors. It could be anyone in that position - your coworker, your neighbor, or the cashier in your local grocery store. You just never know.

I stand strong for womanhood and with my example, I want to show that you can always find a way to change your life. I want to show you through my personal example how I fought back my fears, what I went through and what I have learned. Maybe my story will seem to you banal at times or maybe my story will inspire some of you, because I am a regular girl just like you are. I am not better than you. I am just like you. If I did it, then it means you can do it too. That's why I am willing to share all my secrets, my wins and my faults.

You never know what life will bring to you next. All I know is that you should trust the Universe and stay optimistic and positive no matter what, and always follow your heart. It is magic when your heart intuitively knows what will make you happy, but your mind and logic always tries to create some obstacles and convince you that it is not possible. Women naturally have the ability to know things through a feeling, as women are built with an emotionally intuitive energy. She can tell things by means of her heart. Men are the opposite. They think logically. That's the difference between men and women. It was meant to be that way. That's why they say that women are from Venus and men are from Mars. But that is also why we have difficulties understanding each other sometimes. We always have that battle between the heart and mind. Who is going to win depends on you!

Confession #4

Let's call him Dave. He came into the salon to keep his cut sharp. He was working on Bay St. (it's the Wall St. of Toronto, Canada). He was young (in his late 20's). Handsome. Rich. He was a promising and talented financial expert. His company was paying for his stay at the Ritz Carlton Suite and he was driving a brand new Lamborghini. So when you are in your 20's, hot and rich - all you're interested in are girls and parties. He always had the VIP tables at the finest clubs of Toronto, models around him and jealous looks from the other guys who wanted to be just like him. But obviously he had talent and his mind worked differently, especially if the big companies were hunting for him. More and more, he was drowning in the party night life. He stopped coming to the salon. I did not see him for 4 months. Out of the blue, I bumped into him on the street.

"Hi!" I heard from behind me. When I turned around, I did not see any familiar faces, only this young guy with messy hair and a beard in a white t-shirt and jeans, who was looking at me.

"Hey..." I replied, not recognizing the person, thinking that I might be talking to myself.

"It's Dave."

So that's when I figured it out. He liked to party. All that time when he was going to clubs, he would post on his Facebook that it would be an awesome party at such club and fill it with people. Then he started doing this for money. He went to various club owners and said, "I will make your club crowded if you pay me a certain amount of money." Dave quit his financial expert position job. He opened his own night club. Then another one. Then he partnered with New York and LA club owners. Now he is making a salary that we can only imagine. Dave turned partying into his new business and he is very successful at that. Always follow your heart.

As you see, sometimes you just need to go against the "good boy/girl" complex. It's when your perfectionism dictates your rules - this is good, this is not.

I made the same mistake. I had a long way to go to become a hairstylist. I went from the resistance of my relatives and friends, who said to me back then, "Girl, are you crazy? What? Hairdressing? You are way too smart to work in the service industry. It's a way to nowhere. You will never be able to make enough money. I am sorry, but you are about to ruin your life." But what can be better than to serve people on an everyday basis and make them beautiful? I think it's brought the biggest happiness and purpose to my life.

I think they don't understand that this is a big part of my life, something that lives inside me and needs to be expressed. That it is my art, my way to make this world beautiful. If you see the thankful eyes of your client at least once, and know that is because of you they are sparkling, then you will understand that you cannot circumvent giving into your trust. If you have the need to make people happy, beautiful and confident, to introduce them to the divine world of art, then you will have so much respect for this profession.

Confession #5

Valerie was in her late 40's. She was one of my regular clients and took good care of herself - always was dressed stylish, with a designer's purse and expensive jewelry. She was married for over 20 years and had two adult sons. She was a stay at home mom and her husband was making good money. So she could afford not to work and live a comfortable life. One day, Valerie came in for her usual hair colour appointment and I barely recognized her - no makeup and big sunglasses that were hiding sad eyes. She could not stop crying and was depressed. She told me that her husband left her for another woman and left her with nothing after so many years of marriage. Poor Valerie. She could not pull herself together. She was betrayed and felt like her world had just been crushed. I felt bad for her and, at the same time, all that I could do was just listen and support her with comforting words. Month after month, she came in to have her hair done as usual.

Let me tell you, I admire this woman. After a couple of months, she pulled herself together and decided to move on. She made the decision to become a real estate agent, took a course, and after some time, she got her license. I remember how hard it was for her - to learn new things, pass exams, and change her whole life. Even during the hair colour process, she would read books and make notes.

When you are in your late 40's and decide to become a professional woman, especially if all of your life you were a stay at home mom, it's not easy. She would ask me how to operate Facebook, and all the other popular social media sites that people were using. It's natural for the younger generation to know that stuff, but not for her. She was stubborn and decided to become an independent professional woman, and damn, she was serious about it.

I admire Valerie. After a couple of years of hard work and an endless learning process, she became a top real estate agent in the most expensive area of Toronto. Now she is a successful business owner, has her own office and her own stuff. Oh, and yes, she has a boyfriend and is very happy in her new relationship. Way to go, Valerie.

Happiness begins with the decision to no longer feel sad. I am not saying it's easy, but it is definitely worth it. I have a right to say that as

I made a 180 degree turnaround in my life. As a hairstylist, I have witnessed all these stories with real people. It's hard to change your life, but NOT impossible. I know what I am talking about. We, women, are much stronger than we think. Sometimes the Universe creates those tough situations in our lives, not to crush us, but to give us an opportunity to rise from the ashes like a Phoenix bird.

I know how hard it is to stay positive, especially when your life is falling apart. But I will stress one more time - every morning when you wake up be grateful for everything you have. Someone once said, "I cried because I had no shoes, until I met a man who had no feet."

I decided to turn fashion and beauty into my profession to be able to help other women feel beautiful on a professional level.

Chapter 2
A Hairstylist Is A Happy And Friendly Person

"And now here is my secret, a very simple secret:
It is only with the heart that one can see rightly;
what is essential is invisible to the eye."
Antoine de Saint-Exupéry, The Little Prince

Every time you walk into a salon, you expect to meet a happy, smiley and friendly hairstylist, who will take care of you and spend the next hour or so concentrating exclusively on you and your look. As a hairstylist, I have no right to be sick, to be upset, and can have no personal drama because I need to treat every client with cheerfulness and to be as clean as a piece of paper. And it does not matter that the previous one was a bitch or that I have a headache or PMS. It is a big psychological pressure. It does not matter if my Mom is sick or I just broke up with my boyfriend, I MUST be friendly and happy, because who is the star? It's not me. It's my client in my chair. Do you know how I handle that pressure? I just simply LOVE what I do. For me, it's my form of meditation, my retreat, my way to forget my everyday problems and be above it. When I create beauty, I touch God.

Confession #6

My colleague Sara is a single mom. She is a very talented girl, very passionate and a hard worker. Her creativity is ahead of the times. Simply superb. As is the case with any artistic person, she was extremely sensitive. Every sarcastic comment from a client was greeted with a smile, but it was wounding her as if it was a sword. Of course, she acted cool and did her job the best way that she could.

When she finished work and went home, her best friend was alcohol. It was a pain killer for her heart, the relief for her sensitive artistic soul. The more she hurt - the worse it got. Cocaine became another great buddy. The combination of them both was just the right recipe to forget the ordinary things that happened during the day and reach Nirvana.

At first, it was fun.

One day, her hands were so shaky in the morning that Sara could not perform a haircut. She screwed up. Then a hair colour was wrong. Then she was fired from the salon. She didn't get any help, so she fell deeper and deeper into the rabbit hole with no exit.

Thank God, her family and friends put her in rehab. Now she is back on track. She is working in one of Toronto's salons and we all can just pray that she will be strong enough not to turn back onto that slippery road.

This situation is not an exception, but most of the time, it has a tragic ending. A lot of young and talented hairstylists did not make it to the top, because they are lost at the beginning of their journey. Pressure sometimes is stronger than the ability to fight back. And it's not the worst case scenario. I have witnessed a world class hairstylist, who was doing hair for Madonna and other A-list stars, end up on the street, homeless with no fame, no money, no help and no future.

Why does it happen? Often we meet people who treat their hairstylist like a tool, not like a person. When clients think, "I paid good money for this service, so it gives me the right to be rude, insensitive and treat the person as help," then that is not right. On my side, I can deal with any kind of person. I am lucky now, because I have a right to choose a client or fire one. But at the beginning, I did not have that privilege - whoever sat in my chair - I had to take that person as a client no matter what. That is a problem not every beginner stylist can deal with.

Confession #7

Melanie was a client of mine for over a year. I transformed her cheap blonde colour into a luxury multi-toned one, improved the health of her hair and made it look like a Hollywood star hairdo. She was divorced, had money and enjoyed her life. But her ex dumped her for a younger woman, so she did not like anybody younger than herself, because she was very insecure. That day, the service was as usual - colour with highlights and a blow out at the end. She was supposed to go on a date with a new man that night, so I tried my best to make her look stunning.

While her colour was processing, she received a message that her date was canceled. Oh my...she was mad.

After I finished blow drying the last section of her hair, she looked very angry. My work was great as usual, but she simply needed to get her anger out. "Who the fuck do you think you are?" She started literally screaming at me. "Why are your prices so high? You are nobody! Do you hear me? You are nobody and your name is nothing. You are a fucking immigrant, who works here to serve me. You are simply worth nothing!"

There is nothing uglier than when a woman is desperately looking for a man. She forgets about her pride, her self-esteem and her loyalty to other women. Everyone in the salon stopped working and was just looking at us.

I felt so bad. I was hurt, and I ran to the back in tears.

Don't take this the wrong way, Melanie is a gorgeous woman, but she is very disrespectful to other people. It's not right to treat your hairstylist or somebody else like that.

Also, don't forget, karma will punish you. So always treat people like you would like to be treated.

After that day, I refused to do her hair and the same was true of every single stylist in the salon. Yes, hairstylists can come together and protect each other, because everyone understands that instead of me, tomorrow it could be anyone from the salon.

I found out later that her blonde hair was fried at another fancy salon with a big name. When she asked my boss to book an appointment with me again, he refused to accept her as a client again. No respect – no hair service.

My name is Anastasia. I am a hairstylist and I am proud of it.

What made me choose this profession and did I always know that I would be a hairdresser?

Have you thought about why people all over the world admire Mona Lisa's smile by Leonardo da Vinci? What did Bach or Beethoven want to express through their divine music? Can you see the story behind every architectural masterpiece? I am excited to watch ballet, listen to opera or read a book. I have tears flowing from the Van Gogh paintings or even a good movie. Have you ever thought about what the world of art actually is?

I know this is not easy. I had a long way to go to make it in this profession. This is the purpose of my life and a source of happiness for me, despite the resistance I initially received from my relatives and friends who thought I was making a big mistake entering the service industry. But I couldn't think of a better way to spend my life than serving others.

I think they don't understand that this is a big part of my life, something that lives inside of me and needs to be expressed. That it is my art, and my way to make this world more beautiful.

I want to show this beautiful world to every single one of my clients in the salon, bringing the art into their everyday life and help them improve their lives, as we all know that your look is a reflection of your inner self.

I want every woman to feel the need to come to the salon, relax, trust the hairdresser and touch the beauty through her hairstyle. It's so important.

At the end of the day, I could be really tired, but I know for sure that I did not waste my time, my day, or my life. As long as I am able to help people feel more beautiful, more confident and important, I know that I am doing everything right.

Being a hairstylist is not easy. We are not only hair magicians, we are also psychologists, family advisors, listeners, and friends. When a person sits in my chair and shares stories from her life, I need to show authentic interest in it. Sometimes women give me information that I am not even supposed to know. Sometimes I pretend that I have listened to them. When a blow dryer is working (and it is very loud) - I cannot hear a thing. Usually I just answer "yeah" or "no way" and hope that intuitively those answers fit right into the conversation and she is not asking for a discount to which I just answered positively.

Sometimes you are involved in drama against your will.

Confession #8

I was booked for a cut and blow dry with this lady. Let's call her Cindy. During her appointment, she was talking about her best friend, Lily. She told me such personal information about her friend's life that I felt uncomfortable. But what could I do? I just performed my service. She told me that Lily's husband was cheating on her with one of their other friends. Their financial situation was not great and they might lose their house. There was no sex life between the husband and wife. Lily was about to lose everything, and she didn't even know that her husband had a mistress. Everybody around Lily knows (now including me) but not her.

What a surprise it was when Lily came to me to have her hair done a couple of days later. She told me that Cindy recommended me as a great hairstylist, so she decided to give me a try. It's that uncomfortable moment when I meet a person for the first time in my life, but I know everything about her, including details of her sex life or lack of one.

I felt so bad for that woman. She is not only about to lose her family, but she didn't even have a real friend to talk to. Her girlfriend was not a real friend to her, because real friends don't gossip behind each other's back with strangers (you could call me a stranger at that time). I could not even tell her anything. I just felt sorry for her and made her experience in the salon the best I could.

But what a shock it was when the mistress came in a couple of days later. As I mentioned, they were all friends. That girl told me that she was having her hair done because she had a date that night. She told me she is dating a man and liked him very much, how great he is, and how he is about to reveal everything to his wife and then they will move in together and so on.

I knew the whole story from behind the scenes. As a woman, I understand that everyone of us wants to be happy, to be loved and to love. I don't know if you can build your happiness, however, while ruining another person's life. I am not judging. Just saying - ladies, be careful whom you call your friend.

That's what I mean. Sometimes the psychological pressure is too great. As for any human being, you feel sorry for other people's problems, but it's not my business to be involved. I just do your hair.

Also, people try to manipulate your feelings and make you feel guilty just to get a discount or a better deal. Instead of saying, "Stop it! You look perfect. Go enjoy your life." You need to find a calm, polite and friendly way to deal with useless complaints that have nothing to do with a hair problem.

What I have noticed over the years in this industry, is that the happier a person is with her life - the more open and more trustful she is to you as a professional hairstylist. And the opposite is also true. The more unsatisfied and unhappy a person is with her life - the more "picky" and difficult client she is. Subconsciously, she tries to put you on her level. "I am going to ruin your day, because I am not happy and you should not be happy today either."

There is another category of clients who really suffer in their lives, those dealing with serious health problems, such as cancer; health issues with their kids; or other beloved ones. Those people are more kind and more understanding. It has no logic and it amazes me.

Confession #9
My Mom had serious health problems. I am so grateful to the Universe (God, Buddha – call it whatever) that she is alive. I was so scared of

losing her and, in order to help other women, in my salon I offered a free haircut if you were donating your hair for wigs for cancer patients. The only condition was - you have to leave your hair with me and I will send it in myself. Once I had a dishonest person who claimed she wanted to cut her hair for women with cancer. Later I found out that she actually sold it to a commercial company who creates hair extensions that have nothing to do with any charity or cancer survivors.

One day, Judy came in to the salon and asked me to cut her hair for a hair donation. She asked if she could take her hair with her. I explained the salon policy. She had no problem paying and then said, "Can I book an appointment with you for my 2 sisters? Our Mom has cancer, so the three of us are going to cut our hair to make a wig for her."
It was a very emotional moment. Of course, I could not charge them. It was a very emotional moment for all of us, but we did it. They donated their hair for their Mom.

What a touching and emotional moment it was when I saw the three of them passing by my salon's big window and waving to me with their Mom in a new wig.

My work is very personal and very emotional at times. Also, it can get very dirty. Any of you who like to come to a sparkling clean salon with freshly washed towels, where all the combs and brushes are clean and sterilized, have you ever thought about who makes sure that it is all done? Yes, hairstylists. We clean toilets, wash floors, sweep up hair, do laundry, clean mirrors and a myriad of other tasks. But the most disgusting thing is when a person comes in with smelly and dirty hair, and you have no choice but to touch it, because you are the one who washes it. And yes, before you even bring her to the sink, you need to check her hair for lice. You will be surprised how many people have them. Moms who have school aged children are especially considered high risk clients. But I still love my job.

Another thing that happens frequently, and that I have zero tolerance for, is when a client is sick with the flu, another virus or even pneumonia, but still comes in for their service. They sit in the chair coughing, sneezing and spreading germs around, but still expect you to provide the service. Guys, if you are sick - please stay home.

Hairdressers are also people who can get sick. It is just disrespectful in my opinion. Also, remember that I am not getting paid for sick days. So I can't afford to risk my health and money, just to be there for you.

Another thing - holidays. We're always working on holidays to make you look your best, so be nice to us (hairdressers). Instead of cooking turkey for Christmas Eve, we perform blow dries all day and our shoulders are killing us, but we keep going as we really love what we do. New Year's Eve? Sure! We start really early in the morning and keep running all day and then, with no nap in between, we rush home to shower, put on makeup and are able to party all night. How is that possible? Because we are rock stars and the adrenaline from the job just makes everything spin around.

I truly believe that hairstylists are some sort of magicians, rock stars and artists. We make you feel good about yourself (or sometimes bad!), we raise your self-esteem, make you feel pretty, chat when you are in a good or bad mood and treat you like the most important person in the world, especially when you are in our chair. We are like a version of Superman - we can fix you and make you look your best.

Unfortunately, in this industry, we also have a lot of not so great hairstylists. I am sure you have had a bad experience at least once during your lifetime. Sometimes it has nothing to do with the technical skills of the hairdresser. French women say - it's harder to find a good hairstylist then a good husband. In some respects, this is true. If you think about it, the hairdressing industry is not that big. Chances are that your new hairstylist knows your previous one. To see if your new stylist is a good person, let him/her speak about other stylists' work, or even worse - if your stylist is discussing other clients with you - be sure he/she is talking about you too. I call them "diva"-dressers or "drama"-dressers, not hairstylists. I never let myself be involved in gossip. But I was a witness to many times when it did happen. Another disrespectful thing to do is read the client's emails or texts over their shoulder and then discuss it in the back room with others. Be careful of these types of dishonest stylists.

Many times, I would see a hairstylist chit-chat with you and act like your friend, but as soon as she reached the staff room, she would laugh and gossip about you. Then they would come back to you and act like your friend again. That's why I am stressing this - don't talk about personal things. Remember, a hairstylist is a professional whom you hired to do a job for you – a hair service. I am sure you would not discuss your personal issues with your doctor, dentist or accountant, so why would you do this with your hairstylist?

I have an explanation of why it is so easy to talk to your stylist. Usually they look happy and friendly, so it is easy to pour out your heart. But is it true? Of course, if you come in for haircuts with the same person for years and bring your kids, then it's okay if your hairstylist asks how are they doing at school, but it's not OK to talk about your sex life or your friend's issues. I understand it's so easy to feel comfortable around your hairstylist. You do need to trust the person who works around your head with toxic chemicals and sharp objects, like a razor or scissors, someone who is touching your body, but you also need to use your common sense.

Chapter 3
School - Why Education Is So Important

"Education is the most powerful weapon
which you can use to change the world."
Nelson Mandela

Depending on the level of success that you're seeking to achieve, the level of education may not be relative, but the bottom line is an education of some sort is often paramount to future success. Completing increasingly advanced levels of education shows that you have a drive and commitment to learn and apply information, ideas, theories, and formulas to achieve a variety of tasks and goals.

Education develops our minds. We become better students as we work to understand all the subjects of our study. We have the increased ability to understand our social rights and duties. Due to education, we can understand the difference between right and wrong. Through education, we also understand our religious or spiritual values and standards better. Educated people make an educated nation. Education helps us to open our minds and to improve ourselves.

Millions of illiterate people live in darkness. Education removes this darkness. Education is necessary for the success of every field and sector. We take good care of our costly things because we are aware that they could be lost or destroyed. Education is the only thing that can't be stolen or taken away from us. That's why you can't be a cheapskate when it comes to your education. It's the best investment of your time, effort and money.

Do you want to make the Earth a better place to live? Remember, that education has played a major role in the evolution of modern life for all individuals in society. It has enabled societies to prosper both socially and economically, simply by enabling them to develop a common culture and values.

The most important thing that education brings is confidence. Nothing in this life can be achieved if you don't believe in yourself. Education is what brings self-confidence out in us. We get that confidence from doing things on our own, through gaining new skills and training. Our self-confidence then helps us in passing through all the difficulties that come our way.

Also, education is not a constant unit. It's like a foundation on top of which you are always layering more knowledge, expertise and experience. The more educated you are - the more curious you become about other things. You just can't stop learning. Here is where self-education comes into your life. An academic education is just the basic stuff, what makes you stand out in the crowd is self-education.

"School education isn't the end to your education. Living up to your true potential can only come by continuing to self-educate yourself for as long as you exist." - said Edmond Mbiaka, and I agree with that.

For example, in hairdressing school every student was taught how to cut hair, but not every hairstylist is a good cutter. At school, they teach us the basic techniques and skills. To improve on them, I took more courses and watched other masters' work. Don't forget that we are living in a time when technology makes it easier to access any information in the world, so I was able to see how hairstylists work in Japan, Australia, and Europe. Here self-education comes in its most powerful form, but you need to have discipline and a desire to learn and invest time in yourself.

Education is more than just reading, writing, and arithmetic. It is one of the most important investments an individual can make in his/her future, and it is critical to reducing poverty and inequality. Let me explain why I think so.

Have you ever thought about why a good education is always so expensive? Because knowledge that transforms your life can't be cheap. Imagine a world without any schools and colleges! Impossible, right? No matter how much you hate waking up early for school or studying all night in preparation for those tests and exams, you all know that an education is very important. Now, I am not saying that an uneducated man has no chance of being successful or that an educated man will surely do well in life. Exceptions always exist. However, most of you will agree that the educated person is offered better opportunities in life. It is easier for him to become successful and realize his dreams, compared to someone who is uneducated. Other than success and economic prosperity, there are a variety of reasons why education is a necessity in today's world.

Education gives people the critical skills and tools needed to help them better provide for themselves and their children. However, education is very important to both your personal and professional life. Why? Simply because the skills to analyze and define what is important to you will become almost secondary nature, giving you the ability to understand books, people, and life on a deeper level. But education has nothing to do with personal morality. Let's not mix up these two things. I've met morons in my life with the best education in the world and the kindest people who could barely read and write.

I've attended an art school and have two University diplomas (teacher and psychologist). On top of that, I graduated from beauty school. All that was done before I was 30 years old. You might say - it's impossible. I would say - everything is possible for a curious mind.

Edmond Mbiaka also said, "There is a big difference between school education and self-education. School education has some limits to it, but self-education doesn't. So in order to unleash your greatest potential in life, you must effectively combine the two. Self-education is one of the strongest pillars in the mind of every great person because it is an ongoing process that never ends." It is a never ending process of intellectual growth. That is where your power is. No matter where you start, with self-education you only become better. It's the progress of improving your life.

For example, I always take any opportunity available to improve my skills as a hairstylist. When I am going on a vacation, I always check to see if that city has some hairstyling courses or seminars going on. Over the years, I have been in many countries and have learned different techniques, secrets and tips from hairstylists all over the world. That's what makes me different, plus years of experience. It does not matter what your field of expertise is, it's always the right time to get better and learn more.

What is the difference between talent and skill? Talent is your natural ability, which is inborn. Skill is a learned ability. It is acquired or developed after you put in a lot of time and hard work. The difference between talent and skill is hard work.

It is clear that both talent and skill go hand in hand. A skill can be easily learned through dedication and hard work. One can learn to execute a skill. However, if this task is done without talent, it will not be unique. As a result, you will continue to live in mediocrity. Where the grey area resides is in people's perception of what their 'talent' really is. It usually takes external observations or opinions to help guide one towards what they are truly talented at.

Education is very important but that doesn't guarantee the talent. Absolutely not, but what it can guarantee is the more experience and education you have, the greater the chances are that your hairstylist is very good and talented. It's not just a vision. It's a mix of confidence, your technical skills and your vision. You need to be creative to know that you are performing well and, more importantly, you need an education to know HOW to do it. You cannot paint a painting without knowing how to paint. To have a good and talented hairdresser, you need to make sure he/she is well educated and trained by the best mentors and teachers. Now you understand why education is so important. As I explained before, it costs a lot of money. That's why your hair cut and your hair colour are not cheap, especially if you want quality and skill. If you opt for cheap, then you get what you pay for in terms of skills. Of course, here and there we have some exceptions, but most of the time, it is like that. Talent is really equal to the skills, education, experience, passion and vision of your hairstylist.

From a young age, my parents instilled in me the importance of hard work and dedication. Along the way, I have made mistakes and even changed the direction I wanted to go with my career. From childhood, I wanted to pursue a career as a hairdresser, but was forced to go to

University. After finishing my education, I decided to switch directions and do something I was passionate about. From a young age, I had a passion for the arts, beauty and style. I finished hairdressing school at 27 years old. I was old compared to students right out of high school. I did not have the luxury of taking things slowly or wasting my time. I was constantly learning. This is the secret of my success. When you have passion, drive, talent and a professional education on top of that - you are unstoppable.

Confession #10

My father is an artistic person. He is a musician. When I was at school, he used to work as a music teacher as well. For my younger sister and I, attending an art school was a no-brainer. My parents enrolled me in art school when I was 8 years old. To say that I hated it is an understatement. When my classmates were playing in the yard, I had to go to art school. We had no car, so it took me 40 minutes to walk one way. No matter the weather, I had to go there and spend at least 3-4 hours, instead of having fun with my friends.

We were studying the history of art, painting, sculpture, music, opera and more. One of the tasks was to learn how to play a musical instrument of my choice. My parents wanted me to choose the piano, but I thought, "If you guys are going to torture me, then I am going to choose whatever I want." Drums sounded just right. As a rule, you needed to practice at home. My parents threatened me with the death penalty and told me to choose something else. Then I chose the violin.

You have no idea what a horrible noise a violin can make if you don't know how to play. Very soon, not only were my parents, younger sister and the dog, but even our neighbors, were hiding when I pulled the violin out of my case.

Seven years later, when I got my diploma of secondary education, I also got a certificate for finishing art school.

I have no regrets what so ever. That education gave me an idea about the basics of understanding and composing music; understanding the styles of architecture; the history of paintings, sculpture, opera, symphonies, and more. So now I can enjoy a full Mozart concert and see the beauty in a Michelangelo, and I don't mix up Van Gogh and Rembrandt. I also understand the meaning of words like "renaissance", "neo-gothic", "baroque" or "rococo".

I use that knowledge in my hairstyling every day. That is what makes me unique. As my clients say - she has a vision.

Sure. It took me seven bloody years to learn that stuff, but now I am very thankful to my parents that they pushed me to finish art school.

If you think you are done learning when you graduate from hairdressing school, you are so wrong. They teach you just the basics. All the extras you need to learn by yourself. Constantly, you heard it right CONSTANTLY, upgrade your skill level and education. The day when a hairstylist thinks that he/she knows everything, then it's time to put the scissors down and retire from that career.

In the 21st century, we are blessed with the Internet, giving us access to online courses, YouTube videos and tutorials, as well as hands-on seminars and classes where professional hairstylists can be trained and guided. There are so many of them - updo, colour, cut, barbering and more. On top of that, you need to know other stuff, such as marketing, social media, psychology and the list could go on and on. It's not cheap to upgrade yourself all the time, because those classes can cost hundreds, sometimes thousands of dollars. If the class is in another city or even another country, then you need to pay for your flight, hotel, and food expenses on top of your class costs. It's expensive, but absolutely a must for every hairdresser who wants to be on the top of his/her game.

Let's talk a little about YouTube tutorials. They are so popular among clients. Well, it could be a good thing, but it could be an absolute disaster.

I don't mind that you watch those videos on styling and blow drying your hair. Sometimes they can be really useful for girls without any hairdressing education. They can also showcase ideas on how to create a simple style based on your hair type, or an easy way to style your hair in minimum time. But please use your common sense.

Before using a flat iron or curling iron, consult with your hairdresser on what temperature is suited for your hair texture, how long it should be used, what products to use and how you should use them to keep your hair healthy, shiny and gorgeous. For example, Asian hair texture is very different from super curly, and coloured hair should be treated differently than virgin hair. That's why you should use common sense when you are watching those demonstration tutorials on YouTube that are not made by professional hairdressers. It's good to watch just to get idea about what to do with your hair on an everyday basis, or sometimes a hairstyle can inspire you to create your own. But when it comes to hot tools or products, please consult with your hairstylist. I am sure your stylist will be happy to help you and educate you on how to style your hair on your own.

YouTube

Now I would like to talk to you a little more about YouTube, because YouTube tutorials are very popular today. A lot of girls and women, like you and me, are just using this tool to see what is going on in the industry, if there are new products out, for new styles or new trends and other stuff like that. It can be a really good thing, because it can inspire you to create your own style or just get inspired to look beautiful every day or get an idea of how to work with your hair every day. But you should be very conscientious and use common sense when it comes to hot tools or hands-on tutorials.

It's better just to discuss your plan with your hairdresser, because we all have different textures of hair, different lengths, coloured or virgin hair, curly or straight. Every one of these aspects matter to determine what temperature you should use on your hot tools, what products you should use to keep your style, and what is going to make it last longer and hold better. All of those questions matter.

So just use the tutorials for inspiration, but don't follow their full instructions because usually the videos are not created by professional hairdressers. They are just regular girls who are doing it for fun and not every single experiment is going to be a success story. I have seen many examples where girls have burned their hair with a curling iron or used it the wrong way. For example, let's say they use heat protection spray and then after applying it, they do not let the hair dry completely before using a flat iron. As a result, they burn their hair and then after the hair is ruined, there is nothing that you can do about it, except cut it.

My "favourite" part is the "colouring at home by yourself" tutorials. Usually girls say, "I'm not a professional hairdresser but this is what I did...", or even worse, "My neighbour's friend is a professional hairdresser and this is what she told me to do..." and I'm looking at those video tutorials and it is like a horror movie. I was like, "Wait! Wait... What are you putting on your hair? Oh no. No way. Oh my God! Oh my ..." It is really terrifying for me, as a professional hairstylist, when I see girls using chemicals, not even thinking about the results and what they can do. They are lucky if they still have their hair on their head and not in the sink. You have no idea how many bad cases I've seen over the years. So many girls have done that to themselves at home, then come and ask me to fix it.

The worst case scenario was when one person came in with a bald section on top of her head and bald patches all over the rest of her head. Why? Because she had chemically burned her scalp and the follicles of her hair. They never grew back and she became bald because she burned her skin so deeply. It was a certain degree of burn and when it's done, there is nothing that you can do about it but wear a wig. Even to put extensions on, you still need to have at least some hair.

Now let me tell you this story.

Confession #11
A client, let's call her Clara, came into my salon and told me:

"I was trying to get blonde from black. I was trying to get rid of a black box colour..." *Then she took her hat off. OMG! Her hair literally had every single colour of the rainbow spectrum. It had orange, red, yellow, white, green, brown, and any single colour that you can imagine. To colour correct that mess was going to cost a fortune, because I needed to take it strand by strand and fill those spots with the right colour and then colour it all at once. There is not a miracle that exists that you are going to slap all over the head and have it turn out a beautiful and*

equal colour. The worst thing was that she had her ponytail in her hand. She took out the ponytail from her pocket and asked, "Oh, and this hair just felt out. Can you reattach it? Because I had long hair before and now it is shoulder length and I want it back." The ponytail was white. It was bleached all over and felt like cotton. There was nothing that I could do about it, except throw it out.

Clara ended up with a pixie cut. In my opinion, she was lucky, because at least she had not burned her skin, so new hair will grow back. Why should you take these risks with your beauty? Because you thought you were educated enough by those tutorials that you could do it at home.

Professional hairdressers have received a professional education. It takes a long time and costs a lot of money. For example, in Canada, it takes from ten months to a year. Every day from 8 am to 5 pm, you need be present at school to get your basic hairdressing diploma. Then after that, you have to keep constantly upgrading your education. That's why if it was that easy to just change your hair colour at home, it would never take so long to study and learn these techniques. Please remember - chemical services are so dangerous that even professional hairstylists can screw up sometimes. So if you don't know what you are doing - don't do it.

Colour, straightener, relaxer and perm, and any other chemical services are very dangerous in the hands of the uneducated. Even professional hairdressers can make mistakes and can damage your hair. If it was that easy, then the hair industry itself would be dead, because everyone would be doing it at home. Instead, the industry has spent millions of dollars creating new products and gentler chemicals with scientific input. I can't stress it enough, professionals have the training and this is not something that should be do-it-yourself!

How can you know if your hairstylist is always updating and upgrading her or his education? Just ask at some point during your next appointment, even before you schedule your first appointment, what was the last class or course that they took in hair dressing and that is going to answer your question. There are a lot of hair dressers who have not completed one course, not even one class, after they finished school. Of course, they gained experience over the years by doing the same hair cut over and over again. But if you don't learn something new, you just keep doing the same procedure and its boring. That is why Hollywood hairstylists are so different from other hairstylists, because they are constantly learning. Constantly learning is like regenerating your own creativity and regenerating your own talent. Sometimes it is not even that you learn something new, but you have an idea of how you could do it in a different way or which client would be the best suited for that particular hair style or cut. This is how you generate new ideas. Plus, don't forget that in the 21st century, new technology and products come out almost every single day. To be up to date and to know what it's all about, you constantly need to learn, to search for those companies or other educators, even from other hairdressers, but it is a non-stop learning experience.

In the next chapter, you will find out what you are actually paying for in the salon.

Chapter 4
Money - What Am I Paying For?

*"What is a cynic? A man who knows the price of everything
and the value of nothing."*
Oscar Wilde

You are paying for a great service and a relaxing time. It might look very easy and effortless, but the reality is that behind that easy looking work is a lot of training, thousands of hours of experience, many mistakes and plenty of lessons learned.

Beauty school costs thousands of dollars, then after being an assistant, additional training in the salon for a couple of years. After the investment of more money and time in training, you may be working on the floor as a junior stylist. After being an assistant, this is a big step forward in your stylist career. It's going to only go up from here.

You, as a client, are paying for a happy experience in the salon. The more experience a stylist has - the higher the prices are for her services, as the chances that your hair will not look like you want it to are very minimal. An experienced stylist will always ask you what you want, will suggest the things that will work the best with your style and hair type, and educate you to style your hair at home so you can maintain that fabulous look as if you are the stylist's walking advertisement. Even if it looks like your stylist did only a trim and it looks so easy, you are paying for the knowledge and experience of more than hundreds and hundreds of previous cuts. You are paying for the guarantee that you will be able to manage your hair at home and style it accordingly. That your hair will be very easy to deal with on an everyday basis. Stylists already know how to cut, what angle to place the scissors at, what techniques to use to achieve the best results on your hair and how it would be different for hair that is curly, straight, wavy, thick, thin and more.

As a magician showing off a trick, it looks so easy, but do you realise how many hours, months and years of training are behind that masterfully beautiful job? Hairstylists are hair magicians. You will not remember what your bill was at the salon, but you will remember all those compliments that you will get on your hair and that awesome feeling of fabulousness.

The prices in the salon are formulated according to the cost of shampoo, products, rent, economy, time efficiency and other factors. Prices are not created out of the blue. It has some management put into it. So if you book your service with a master stylist - be ready to pay accordingly. Don't be too shy to ask for the prices before you book your appointment.

Confession #12

She was a young, fit, beautiful blonde in her late 20's. She had been coming to the salon for a couple of years, so she was a regular client for my colleague.

She was a very fashionable and stylish lady, who worked out regularly, ate healthy, and regularly visited her cosmetologist and eyelash extension specialist.

After the service was complete, her bill was always the same, as she always did the same thing - full head of highlights, cut, deep moisturizing treatment and a blow out at the end.

During the process, she would mention that she had bought a new Prada purse, or the jeans from the latest Diesel collection, or a limited edition pair of Louboutin shoes. Or she was telling us what luxury trip she had just come back from.

The end of the service also was always the same. "My purse/shoes/trip were so expensive, my credit cards are over the limit and my debt is over 100k, so can you give me a discount? Please, give me a discount."

It's not cool, because it's very disrespectful to the stylist. My colleague is a single mom who does her best to deliver a high quality level of service to her clients. Her time costs money. If you need to be on a budget sometimes, ask for a junior stylist who has prices that are cheaper, or better manage your shopping and credit card payments. A client's financial situation is not a stylist's problem.

It means she is trying to save money on her stylist, but not on her shopping. In reality, it means she is asking for permission to steal the stylist's money. That stylist has expenses too, she has a kid and bills to pay. When the client is asking for a discount, it means she is trying to take away the money that the single mom might be spending on her kid. A stylist's time is money and if the client tries to steal money from the stylist, it means she has no appreciation and respect for her stylist.

Of course, there are times when you need to be on a very strict budget. I had a client for many years and it just so happened that she lost her job and was in the process of finding a new one, when her dad died. She called me to ask for a solution. She asked me if there any mass market colours that would match her existing one and she asked if a junior stylist could do a blow out on the day of funeral. I knew that lady very well, and after hearing what she was going through, I offered to do her hair for free. Yes, stylists have a sensitive side, and for loyal clients, we can move mountains when they are in a tough situation.

Sometimes people will try to commit fraud. For example, I remember I had a walk-in client. After a colour and cut, it was time to pay. She told me that she was going around the corner to get the cash, because for some reason, she didn't want the hair service to be on the bank statement. In escrow, she left her Louis Vuitton purse. Later, I discovered it was a cheap fake copy of a Louis Vuitton bag stuffed with newspaper.

I would like to talk to you about respect. You might say, what? I'm always respectful to my hair stylist, what do we have to talk about? But there are a couple of things, which in a hairstylist's eyes, look very disrespectful. For example, when you're running behind and you know that you are going to show up late, but don't let us know. Hairstylists book your time exactly based on the service that you requested. So time is very important, since it is the schedule from one client to the next one that can be disrupted when you are late. Either it means I need to cut off your service or I provide the full service that you requested and I will be late for the next client. This is disrespectful to the client who was on time. It can throw a stylist's whole schedule off for the day.

Please find a way to inform your hairstylist that you will be late. Sometimes this means that we will have to reschedule you. There is no way I can start your haircut if I have only 20 minutes left of your time. I'm not going to provide a quality cut and then you will be unhappy with the service. I'm not the person who is going to do it just halfway. I want to do the full service, so if you are really running late, just please inform your stylist and let's reschedule.

Another thing that is disrespectful is when you are running late and you call to say you are running late, but show up with a fresh cup of coffee from any of the assorted coffee shops, such as Starbucks or Tim Hortons. You could have spent those 10 minutes in the chair, but instead, you showed a lack of respect for my time and the next client after you, who I will now be late for. This is a real turnoff to any stylist! Another thing would be tips. I hear occasionally that because I own the salon, they aren't going to tip me. If you don't want to tip me, that's fine. Just pay for your service and I'm totally cool with that, but don't give me those types of excuses. It is really unnecessary.

I'm not going to love you any more or less if you tip me or not. Your service will be the same high quality service I always provide. You pay for my service based on what it costs. I spent my time on education. I used my creativity and talents. I am consulting you. I am advising you. I'm working for my money.

It's totally cool if you are not going to leave any tips, but if you decided to tip, please do it mindfully. It's very humiliating when your bill comes to, let's say hundred dollars, and you leave a tip of 88 cents. It's better to not tip at all, because this is insulting to me.

I will perform my work the best that I can. My work doesn't rely on tips. Why does 88 cents on a 100 dollar service look so bad? Just because it means that to you, my effort to make you happy, my vision and my creativity was only worth 88 cents out of 100 dollars. Stop it.

If you don't have money or you're on a tight budget or you simply don't want to tip your stylist, that's totally cool. Just don't humiliate me with a couple cents. Just don't do it.

It looks cheap. It looks like you are not really grateful. You are just demonstrating that you do not appreciate your stylist's work, so again, just don't do it.

I also had one stranger who walked in my salon and asked me if I could trim her fringe. I told her, "Sure. Yes, I can." So I trimmed her fringe and she was happy with the result, it turned out exactly as she wanted. So she was very pleased. I'm here to do my job the best way I can as a hairstylist. Then she took her stuff, her purse and her jacket and just walked straight to the door. I was forced to tell her, "Excuse me, ma'am, but it costs 5 dollars. Would you please pay your bill?" She told me, "Why? It's only fringe."

Let me explain something to you. It might look to you, as a client, that it is very simple and easy to trim a fringe, but you also know how easy it is to screw it up - cut too short or too long or too bulky, too wispy or whatever and it is too much for you. To get it exactly right takes a lot of practice, a lot of experience and a lot of time to learn. Most hairstylists do not charge a lot for a fringe cut or may not charge at all, but at least be nice and offer to pay for it.

Usually, a stylist offers a free fringe trim to regular clients, since a stylist wants her loyal clients to be happy and to reward their loyalty. That's what I do between visits. I trim the fringe for free, but it doesn't mean if you walk in off the street that you get the same treatment for free. There is nothing for free, because my scissors cost money. My electricity costs money. My space where I'm working is rented and my time is money. Be respectful of that.

Another point that I want to talk about is dirty hair. Yes, when you come in for a hair appointment with a colour appointment, you don't need to have freshly washed hair or very clean hair, because I need to have that barrier of natural oil on your scalp to protect your skin from your colour service. But at the same time, it doesn't mean that your hair should be so oily that you can squeeze that oil right onto the frying pan.

When you are coming in for a cut, colour or something else and you know that your hair will be washed, it's totally cool. Of course, nobody expects you to come in with freshly washed hair and a nice blowout or something. But everything in moderation, so have some common sense. When your hair is so dirty that your stylist needs to wear gloves to touch it, this is absolutely unacceptable.

Sometimes a stylist will meet a client who is never happy with their work. No matter what the stylist does - something will be wrong. But the client still keeps booking appointments with the stylist and keeps complaining - too short/too long, too bulky/too wispy, or too light/too dark. Even if you agree to everything before you start working on her hair, there will still be issues. The reason for that behaviour is because they are trying to get a discount or even make you work for free. They just have that type of personality. Unhappy people will never be happy with their hair. Or they will ask you to cut the fringe, then the next time it will be just the sides a little bit, then the next time it will be, "I think my hair is not equal in the back". Such a client will never schedule a full haircut, just a blow dry or colour, as over a couple of visits she gets the haircut, just done partially, a little bit at each visit for other services.

Finally, I would like to talk about cell phones. I understand that we're living in the 21st century where technology is around constantly. We are all attached to our cell phones. They are like extensions of ourselves. When a stylist is working on somebody's hair, whether it is a cut or it is a blow-dry, and the client asks you to stop because she needs to take a call, this is where respect comes in. I am trying to stick to a schedule and do my job at the highest level of quality possible. As a woman, as a human being, I understand if it is an emergency with your family or your kids checking in, but when you are just chatting with your friends - it's not cool. Quick replies are one thing, but long discussions about the Oscars, Instagram pictures or Taylor Swift's outfits are just annoying, not to mention they can make an impact on my time as well. Simply put, I am standing and waiting for you to finish. In the meantime, I will be late for my next client, which is disrespectful to me and to them.

I'm also not enjoying my work, because I can't concentrate on my work. It is already turned down, because as a hairstylist, I'm an artist. I'm creating my masterpiece on your head and it's not just hair, it is your look. It is your appearance. It is how you are presenting yourself to the world and a stylist is helping you with that. You are actually hiring me. You are paying me money for my experience, my talent, my vision to create the best look for you, so it is in your best interest to let me do my work uninterrupted.

There is salon etiquette for both clients and stylists. You can find it in Chapter 7.

But not everything looks so commercial and pessimistic.

Hairstyling is more than a job. It's a vocation. It's a mission. The reason I am being so detailed in this chapter is that I want to explain to people who are visiting a salon as a client, or have a family member or friend who is a hairstylist that this is how it works. Of course, every stylist loves her job, otherwise she would be not able to take so much pressure. It is also a lot of fun. We are creating beauty. We are helping people. We meet new people almost every day. Through chatting with them, we also discover the world and are learning more all the time.

Every single client in a stylist's chair is a unique person, a whole different Universe with her own rules, do's and don'ts, and experiences. In one day, a stylist can meet a housewife, a business woman, a stripper and a writer. Different people are what makes our work exciting.

I am writing this book to explain how the hairdressing industry works from both sides – the client's and the stylist's perspective.

Stylists are usually very soft hearted people and very vulnerable. Of course, it should be that way, as a stylist is touching the hearts of other people by creating beauty for them. Having the ability to see the beauty of a person should make you more sensitive in some ways. Angry people would never accept beauty. Beauty makes you kind.

Sometimes we are harsh to people who we love. Be kind and thoughtful. If your friend is a hairstylist, don't ask for a discount. If you are a real friend, you would understand that it is her job. You should support your friend's career by paying the full price, because maybe she loves you so much that she has no courage to ask for any money, but your friend also has bills to pay. Trust me, this business is not the business where everyone is rich.

Also be mindful that your friend needs a break. The last thing what she wants to do is your hair on her only day off. Your friend would say, "Sure, I can do your hair," just because she loves you. But if you are a real friend, then you will let your stylist friend recharge her battery without talking hair. Yes, every stylist loves her job, but we also need to rest.

Money is important, but love, a smile, friendship, kindness, love, and caring are priceless. They say that the best things in life are free. The second best things are very expensive. Your stylist is 2 in 1.

Chapter 5
I Need You

"Try not to become a man of success,
but rather try to become a man of value."
Albert Einstein

Beauty and sex always go hand in hand. When you come to the salon, of course you expect to leave feeling gorgeous and sexy. Don't you? Well, sometimes it can be too extreme.

Confession #13
The same downtown salon. Don't you love it already? All the "magic" happens downtown. Let's call him Adam. He was a hairstylist, one of our team who always worked late hours. I have to admit, he was hot - body of Apollo and the cute face of Cupid, strong hands, big muscles, tall, in one word – the whole package. He had the most outrageous prices, and no, he wasn't even that good. His shift usually started at 7 pm and lasted till the last client. We never knew his secret until one day one of the hairstylists forget his cell phone and came back to pick it up, discovering Adam on top of this girl. Adam usually hung out in the most popular, prestigious bars and clubs in Yorkville (the hottest area of Toronto). He would introduce himself as an owner of the salon,

even though he was not the best hairstylist in the city. He gave the ladies a business card with his cell phone number and disappeared. Sure enough, sooner or later, they would call him to book a hair appointment with the hottest stylist in the city. And here is how that would play out: "Oh dear. Of course, I remember you. The most gorgeous eyes in the world. How could I forget you? I am very happy that you called. At least I have your number now... (blah-blah-blah... continue putting honey in her ear). I am sorry, but I am fully booked today. But since you are such a special girl, I will work extra hours for you at no extra charge, just because I like you." That's it! Fish is in the net. All of us had a key to the salon, so he would come in whenever he wanted, did average work for the hairdo at top price and accept tips, such as a blow job (don't mix it up with a blow dry). Nice life.

Why am I telling you this story? Just because I want to make a point that not only are you as a client choosing your hairstylist, but the hairstylist also chooses his/her clientele. Having been in this industry for a while, we get that sixth sense of whom we can connect with and perform the best work ever or make big bucks with, and with whom it will be only drama and no productive work. Every hairstylist becomes a psychologist over the years. Because there are times, no matter what you do as a professional, where it will not be good enough. When a client comes in for the first time and says, "Nobody can give me a good haircut, maybe you can do it right," or "All those hairdressers did not understand what I want." That is a big red flag. Get rid of her right away for couple reasons:

1. She is cheap and is always going to want discounted prices. She will never be satisfied with the quality of your work (even though you only have half an hour per head), plus she will complain at the end that your work costs too much.

2. It is highly unlikely that over the years she did not find a stylist who can work with her type of hair.

3. There are a lot of talented hairstylists in this industry at any price range. That means she is just not happy with herself, and you can never, I mean never, satisfy her. When a person is not happy about her life or herself, no matter what you do, she is never happy.

4. Mental issues.

What does that mean? Fire her as a client right that moment. Yes, we fire clients as well.

Sometimes the best hairdresser is not necessarily the best skilled and most experienced hairdresser. We know so many hairdressers who have kind of a Diva complex, such as "Oh my God, I'm so cool", and "You are very privileged to be in my chair." Nobody likes that. Everybody likes the simple, easy going, funny and professional hairdresser. Your experience as a hairdresser and your talent doesn't really matter if you are an asshole. But if you just know what you're doing, are passionate about what you're doing, if your life is just about your industry and about hair, and about making people beautiful because you want to make them happy, then you can find success in this industry. When a person feels good, she is happy, she is smiling, and she feels that she has the power to do anything. A hairdresser can change your life or can even ruin it. Just to do it right, you need to choose the right hair dresser. And how to do that? You can just go by simple intuition, by feedback from other clients or your friends and family or you just try them out. I told you before what French women say, to find a good hairstylist is harder than finding a good husband.

What is the best way to find a hairdresser, who can make your hair look the best? There are a couple of options. First, there is a classic hair salon; second, you can choose any hair dressing school where a student can do your hair; or third, go to somebody's home and do hair there. Let's see examples of these options' pros and cons.

A classic hair salon usually means the hairstylist is licensed, which is really good, because it means if something goes wrong you are going to have insurance and all the chemicals and colours out of there to fix it. It provides more security.

Hair dressing school, on the other hand, is way cheaper, but at the same time, you need to be prepared that not everything will go smoothly. They are students and they can make mistakes as part of the learning process. You are essentially one of their guinea pigs. Yes, there are teachers supervising the students, and it is way better than doing it yourself obviously, but it's not the best way. Still, in some cases, it is an option.

The third way is to do your hair at somebody's home or at a home based salon in a basement. I don't recommend this way because, first of all, there is no guarantee the person is licensed. Who knows, maybe she was disqualified or her license was suspended and now she is doing this at home. Plus, if something goes wrong, there is no guarantee that it will be safe or that you're going to have insurance or your money back. Secondly, I don't really see how it can be as relaxing, because when you are going to someone's home, the hair process will be disturbed by the home stuff. Hearing the telephone ring, maybe they are cooking something so there is the smell of the food, and maybe there are kids running around. It's not an atmosphere where you can relax and enjoy the experience of a nice hair salon and have your hair done professionally. Yes, it's way cheaper, but this is not the best way. You don't know that person and you are at their home. It's not like in a salon where a stylist completely focuses on giving you the best hair style and gives you that feeling that you are special, the way that you deserve.

Every hairstylist needs clients. So it doesn't matter how talented a hairstylist you think you are, or how good you are at hairdressing. The only thing that matters is if you are busy as a hairstylist. Essentially, if you are booked or not. Your success counts only if you are fully booked with clients and if you are busy. So to get to that point, you need to let people know that you exist and let them know that you are good at what you do. So where do you start?

When I finished hairdressing school, obviously I had just a couple of friends that I was doing their hair. That was pretty much it. To get started, you need to build a solid clientele. How to do it? There are actually a couple ways.

First is using social media. Platforms, such as Facebook, Instagram, Twitter, LinkedIn, etc., are powerful tools. You can let people know that you are a hairstylist. Start building your portfolio, taking pictures that are good examples of your work and posting them online. Create an album and just post it there. When people are looking for a hairdresser, then you can direct them straight to your album and show them: "Hey, look this is the work that I have done. If you like it, just come in and book your service."

Another way to get the word out is through online reviews. This is like a referral, just not by traditional word of mouth. People who have used your service leave great reviews about you, then other people are going to read them and they are going to say, "Hey, that's exactly what I want." Or, if you got an unfavourable review, at least you can learn from your mistake. You will know what your weak point is, so you can work on it and fix it. The next time, your clients will just be blown away with the quality of the work that they received from you.

Another thing is communicating with your clients. We're working in a business where we need to deal with people. When it comes down to it, professional skills and experience are great, but nevertheless, what is also very critical is how you communicate with your client. First of all, listen. Listen to what they say. Listen to what they want because when a person says that she wants to be blonde and have a haircut with long layers, there are plenty of options available. Blonde can be a level nine, a level ten, dirty blonde, golden blonde or platinum blonde. There are so many varieties, so it is better to use a visual picture and show it to her. If you are a client, show your hairdresser exactly what you want. If you are a hairstylist, just do a double check. Just use Google, everybody has a smart phone, and find some pictures to show your client to see if that is the style that she is looking for. And when it comes to the cut, sometimes I have heard people say, "Oh...I want these long layers," but at the same time, if you're going to have long layers, short layers, front layers or whatever, you need to explain how to blow dry it. You know that she, as a client, is going to walk out of the salon looking like a superstar. But the next day, when she washes her hair and tries to style it by herself, it's never going to look the same. Before you start cutting, just explain how much time she will need to spend every day or every time she washes her hair to get that look, especially when it comes to the fringe.

When the person has never had a fringe before, and it's the first time that she gets a fringe, overnight it can look not as neat and pretty as it does just freshly blow dried. So just make sure you clear out all those misconceptions before you pick up the tools and start to proceed with your service.

Referrals. I love referrals because it shows that a person loves my work and she is proudly wearing my hair style. Everything is working between us. We have a great chemistry. We have a great understanding between us and all is good. When you're recommending me as your hairstylist to your friend, just keep something in mind. It might not work between me and that other person, who you know on a personal level. Maybe we just have a different vision of beauty, because we are all human beings with unique perspectives.

We attract clients based on that vision of beauty, the same way a client attracts her hairdresser. I told you before what French women say, that to find a good hairstylist is harder than it is to find a good husband. That is so true, because so many aspects should match between your two personalities - vision, creativity and understanding of what is beautiful and so on. So I had this client, let's name her L and she was pushing me as a hairstylist to have her friend as a client. She would say, "Oh my God, she is the best! If you were not in her chair, it means that you've never had a good haircut." I mean come on, there are a lot of talented hairstylists around. Maybe you are not suitable for that particular person and that's it, end of story. At the end of the day, the client's friend called me for an appointment and her expectations were way too high. They were literally unrealistic. This did not turn out well. She was not happy with her hair style and then she started bad mouthing me. It got even worse. Since that friend knew that L came to me for regular appointments, she would start saying, "Oh my God, your hair looks awful. Oh my God, that fringe looks like a dead animal tail," and other bad things.

So be respectful about somebody else's vision and their feelings, because maybe your friend's hairdresser is also very cool, just different from yours. Don't push. It doesn't mean that your friend's hairdresser is better or worse than your hairdresser, just different and be respectful of that.

Another thing, clients think sometimes that they can be rude and bitchy in your chair just because you are hungry for a job. You're obviously working because you want money. So they think they can do whatever they want, because you are here to please them. Here is the truth. Sometimes hairstylists will fire clients as well. There are people that no matter what you do, you are never going to please them. Just absolutely never, and in my opinion, this based on some psychological history. If a person is not happy with her life, she never will be happy about her hair. Something will always be wrong.

This one little strand is too short, this is a little bit long, but it doesn't matter what you do - something is always wrong. It's okay to just focus on those clients with whom you have a good vibe, who is going to recommend you to their friends and family. The people who are pleased with your work. Clients choose their hairstylists, but hairstylists also choose their clients and that's how you have a solid based clientele come together.

This is not going to happen overnight and this never happens very fast, but if you're good at what you do - focus on that. The number one qualification of your work should be the great, absolutely fabulous job you do and then it comes down to how your personalities match. How you get along together and things like that. Also, if you are a client, make sure you go to a professional, who understands and does hair. The stylist is not your friend. She is not your girlfriend. She is not your psychotherapist, so don't talk too much about personal stuff.

Confession #14

I had a client who would come to me regularly for a haircut and colour services. She loved to talk about personal stuff. If she broke up with her boyfriend, what her boyfriend cooked for her last night, and what they planned on seeing at the movies. I mean it's nice that you trust me so much, but this is not necessarily what I should know. She was that client who talked about those things nonstop, including their bedroom activities, such as what noises he made or what lingerie she wore.

It actually got worse because she started talking about her friend. She told me that her friend doesn't know her husband is cheating on her and everybody knows except the wife. That wife just happened to be a client of mine, so of course, professional ethics meant that I couldn't tell her what the other client had told me.

Privacy is the number one rule in my salon. When a client comes in and I already know what's going on in her life without her permission, it's bad enough. But what was worse is that her best friend told me all that stuff. So be careful when you're choosing your friends and what you say about them in a chair. Eventually, they will find out and it can end your friendship, but also other relationships. The friend did find out about the affair and then she went through a painful divorce.

It was not a pleasant time for her. Her best friend, my client, would tell me every single detail of that client's life as she was going through the divorce. They have financial problems. She was having breakdowns and was so emotional, but she was so stupid because she didn't see it coming. I felt so bad for the woman, because her best friend was badmouthing her, instead of providing necessary support through this horrible time. Support your friend and be there for her when you know she is having a hard time. She was bad mouthing her best friend to a person who only does her hair. Basically, I know everything about the situation, most of which I shouldn't know. Real friends would never do this type of thing to each other. So be careful who you call your friend.

On top of that, I know a lot of hairstylists who actually like gossiping. They can do a haircut or blow dry, and look over your shoulder at your emails or your texts, reading every word. Then they come into the staff room and say, *"Hey, do you know that blonde told that brunette in my chair she is like this and that?"* They share other people's personal lives without permission and show a lack of respect. Never share without that person's permission any of the details about her personal life. This applies to hairstylists and clients alike!

A good hairstylist/client relationship is very important for both the hairstylist and the client. A woman's relationship with her hairstylist is unlike any other. When things are going well, the woman is happy, bright, peaceful, in love, and feels beautiful; but when things go wrong, she feels like her life is a disaster and the world around her is dangerous. It adds a lot of stress and she doesn't know what to do.
It is not a big surprise that the biggest secret to having a successful relationship is about communication. Communication is the key. Regardless of the salon you go to, sometimes it can happen that you end up with an untalented or incompetent stylist, and you just have to switch salons. You are lucky when you have found YOUR stylist, if not - continue looking for The One!

From the other side, you should never be the client from hell. No one wants to deal with a client who is mean, disrespectful, or treats you as a servant. The goal for both (client and stylist) is a long-lasting, healthy relationship between the client, the stylist, and the salon that lasts for years.

Chapter 6
The Truth About Your Beauty

"Fashion is not something that exists in dresses only.
Fashion is in the sky, in the street, fashion has
to do with ideas, the way we live, what is happening."
Coco Chanel

Every woman has her own understanding of beauty. In the world, every one of us is unique. This is a good thing, because could you imagine if everyone was the same? It would be boring. The society where you grew up, your family, your education, your friends, your occupation, your taste in movies and books - everything makes an impact on your perspective of beauty.

What can be beautiful for one person, won't necessarily be acceptable by another. For example, miniskirts and high heels could be a norm for one and not work for another woman. The thing is that you need to know your body type, your complexion, your strong features and emphasize those. If you have good intuition and taste, you can do it yourself. But I think that it is always a good idea to ask for professional advice. Just do a pampering treatment for yourself. For example, consult with a professional hairstylist, professional make-up artist, and professional wardrobe stylist or fashion advisor. Also consider going to a professional photographer, because a photographer will know which are the strongest features of your body and face. It would not only be a fun and an exciting experience, but also a great investment in your look.

Do you know that in the global beauty and fashion/clothing industries, women spend way more money than men? That is why you have such a big variety of beauty products, clothing stores, shoe stores and accessory stores designed for women. Did you notice that usually the women's department is way bigger and has a larger selection then the men's department in a store? Why is it like that? Just because a woman's nature is very different then a man's. More impulsive buyers are women compared to men. Big corporations know it and use it to make more money.

How do you avoid getting lost in this ocean of products for women? For example, the same company produces a number of different varieties of shampoo. Another company also has a big selection of shampoo. So how do you choose a good one? Well, you can buy every single one and try them. In that case, until you find something that works for you, you will spend a lot of time and money. The key to looking good is to use the right products. This is where a professional's help can be useful to you.

It doesn't mean you need to break your bank account to get professional help. You can follow professional make-up artists and professional hairstylists on social media. Big department stores have a makeup department with professional makeup artists who work there as consultants. They will be happy to help you find the right shade of foundation or to help you find the right shade of lip stick and it is free.

Don't ignore YouTube tutorials. A lot of professional makeup artists have a YouTube channel that you are welcome to sign up for, and often, they share very useful tips.

Let's talk about quality. The most expensive product does not always mean the best quality. Cheaper options don't necessarily mean they are bad. You should look deeper and know the ingredients or find them on the Internet and get the general information about the company you are purchasing from.

Why are luxury brands so expensive? Of course, you are paying for the brand, but at the same time, big names have a good reputation for using high quality ingredients. Sometimes cheaper cosmetics can look less than beautiful. We all have seen those smudged eye shadows, runny lipsticks and blotchy foundations. Don't be economical on yourself. It is better to invest in one good product versus buying ten cheap ones.

Now we are living in a time where we have fast changing technologies, fast Internet, fast food and fast fashion. What is fast fashion? Before we had a very strict schedule for fashion designers to present their new collections, usually it was spring/summer and fall/winter- two times per year. Now the mass market clothing stores have a new edition to their collection or a new style of clothes almost every week. Usually it is not expensive and that is why it is very popular amongst consumers. Who can resist the deal buy one get one free or just a t-shirt for five dollars? But is it too good to be true?

When you buy a dress or t-shirt for five dollars, you think it is a very good deal. You don't really care if that piece is going to last for a long time, since it was very cheap. You can afford to buy the t-shirt, wear it once for a party, and throw it out after. Who cares, if it is only five dollars.

To produce the cotton that this t-shirt is made of, first you need to plant the cotton seeds in the field. Cheap means volume, so to make sure that all the seeds are going to grow into a plant, they spray it with a lot of chemicals and no one cares about the chemical pollution. To produce that one cheap t-shirt, it means that cheap labour is used, which very often includes women and children. Usually the whole process, from growing the cotton to manufacturing the t-shirt, takes place in a third world country. That is where cheap labour is used and no legal regulations are enforced.

The big manufacturing factories usually have poor working conditions, no air conditioning and the building by itself is in bad condition. We all know about the tragedy that happened in 2013 in Bangladesh, where an 8 story commercial building named Rana Plaza collapsed. Approximately 2500 people were injured and 700 died. The owner was notified that the building was in very bad condition and the walls had started cracking, but there were no changes made to protect the employees. Since it was the only income for the people of that area, with no legal labour rights, no union, and no government protection, people were forced to go to work. For big corporations, it is a great source of cheap manufacturing for their merchandise. So that five-dollar t-shirt is a bloody t-shirt, where a lot of suffering and damaging health effects from the work are involved. Fast fashion stores try to satisfy their consumers' needs, because if no one would buy it or buy less of it, they would not produce it.

Do you think that is the end of the story? No, because when you throw out that cheap item, it creates garbage and garbage should be biodegradable, but usually a chemical process is needed to break down the garbage. Now you can see the connection between when you buy the cheap stuff, and your personal impact on the pollution of our planet.

What should I do, you ask? My answer is to create your own style. Don't be a follower of the fashion trends, because fashion trends are changing fast. Don't be a follower, be a leader! What I mean by that is just be stylish. When you are buying a lot of trendy items and then that fashion has passed, it means you need to buy new ones and update your wardrobe frequently. Those changes happen way too fast, but style never goes out of fashion. Your look is a message that you are sending to the world and how you want to be perceived, so make it the best that you can. For example, buy quality pieces with good fabric that are going to last you a long time and can combine with other pieces. Just create your basic wardrobe. It doesn't mean it should be big names or designer logos, but it should be good quality, clean looking and stylish. What I do is buy good quality fabric, then draw my own design and ask a local dress maker to sew it for me. In that case, I have created my personal style and I am supporting a local small business. To look stylish, you can make a statement with scarves, sun glasses, and other accessories. There was a project done by a New York girl who wore the same clothes for 30 days, but every day she looked different, as she was playing with her accessories. Accessories can change the whole look. To develop your personal style and taste is a skill, but it is something that you can learn. Following trends is just mindless work.

"Fashion plays a major role in our society. Stand in any line waiting to check out and the covers of magazines exude fashion. Designers have movie stars wearing what they decide the season should call for. Every movie or television program has carefully chosen what look they want to portray. Every ad may not be about fashion, but the clothes are a subliminal way of catching the audience and what they are geared to.

Fashion reaches every corner that you turn. The market reaches the elementary schools as most kids "want to fit in". High school is a great target for young teens who must have what everyone else is wearing. At this age, kids are very self-conscious; they are like that in grade school too. In our society, fashion is a display of what your material wealth is and also people "in the know" are aware of how to dress. The only place people can let their hair down is when they are home alone or with a comfortable mate; that is the time for comfort and grubbies; they even had a fashion role at one point during the grunge era, which still does exist. Depending upon the occasion, people dress up or down and don't forget the accessories, which include shoes. What woman (and most men) do not enjoy the look of shoes? Purses make a statement of wealth or lack of. Why is there costume jewelry? Because not everyone can afford the real thing and people want to look and feel good. Even people with an abundance of money do not always wear real gems, as costume jewelry is about fun and it is reasonably priced. From birth to death, fashion is the utmost. When a new arrival makes the scene, many people throw baby showers and the "oohs and "ahh " of the most darling clothes can melt most hearts. Although death is part of life, it is a solemn occasion and this will be the last fashion statement a person will ever make. Weddings are huge money makers for the fashion industry and people will spend almost their entire lifetime savings for the special day that every little girl; well almost every little girl, dreams of. Fashion moves money, which helps the economy. Fashion separates the classes of society also. There are endless restaurants, social events, and churches where fashion plays a large role. All in all, almost every country has their own fashions that make a statement of a person's wealth and the statement they are making reflects style or a lack of style," said Donna Star, in a piece she wrote in 2015.

Fashion affects the social aspects of life. According to Luciana Zegheanu, fashion causes changes in the social, economic and political landscapes. Thus, fashion benefits and stimulates society, in the process of promoting creativity. Fashion also has negative impacts. For instance, it diverts peoples' attention from other important activities and affects the self-esteem of people who cannot afford certain clothing.

When fashion distracts people, especially youth, from more productive activities, they focus more on acquiring the latest and most fashionable items rather than on their education or work. People who cannot afford certain fashionable items sometimes have diminished self-esteem and do not feel adequate among their peers. At times, people are bullied for not having the latest fashions. Some people believe fashion is harmful, since it creates a society in which appearance is often valued more than character.

On the positive side, fashion is an art, which stimulates and inspires people to express themselves. People often show off their personal identity, talent and culture through their fashion choices. People use what they see on fashion runways and in the stores to create their own unique looks, thus expressing their creativity. Fashion also promotes creativity on the runway, as designers endeavor to outdo one another through their unique and intricate designs.

Here is a quote from a great fashion movie called "The Devil Wears Prada". It shows how fashion affects everyone - even people who don't think they have a sense of fashion, people who refuse to acknowledge fashion, and people who think that fashion is a stupid thing and they are above that. It points out how even someone who puts on an ugly sweater is making a conscious fashion decision, because that is how one is choosing to portray their style to the rest of the world. It is quite impressive.

Miranda Priestly said, "This... 'stuff'? Oh. Okay. I see. You think this has nothing to do with you. You go to your closet and you select... I don't know... that lumpy blue sweater, for instance, because you're trying to tell the world that you take yourself too seriously to care about what you put on your back. But what you don't know is that the sweater is not just blue, it's not turquoise, it's not lapis, it's actually cerulean. And you're also blithely unaware of the fact that in 2002, Oscar de la Renta did a collection of cerulean gowns. And then I think it was Yves Saint Laurent... wasn't it him who showed cerulean military jackets? I think we need a jacket here. And then cerulean quickly showed up in the collections of eight different designers. And then it, uh, filtered down through the department stores and then trickled on down into some tragic Casual Corner where you, no doubt, fished it out of some clearance bin. However, that blue represents millions of dollars and countless jobs and its sort of comical how you think that you've made a choice that exempts you from the fashion industry when, in fact, you're wearing the sweater that was selected for you by the people in this room from a pile of stuff."

Fashion has been around since the beginning of the human race. The definition of fashion, according to dictionary.com, is a prevailing custom or style of dress, etiquette or socializing. The presence, awareness, and preferences of dress in everyday life, whether it was a cave man selecting which pelt to wear on a cooler day, a child living in medieval times choosing their favourite coloured garment, or a fashion designer in today's world selecting fabric for their newest pieces, is fashion. It is a particular preference of how one would like to physically portray themselves that has always been present. This shows that fashion is a long lasting factor in society. Fashion can affect the economy of a country or the whole world. It can sway politics, serve as an art form and can affect someone's personal life. Needless to say, fashion is arguably one of the biggest factors that affects and that can be affected by society. It has always been present and will always be present for as long as the human races exists.

Fashion changes all the time and it can change the perception of women and how women view themselves. Fashion has a bigger impact on women mentally then you think. The fashion industry, TV, fashion magazines - media in general has shaped our culture and blows up the public with its idea of beauty. Women are obsessed over this image that they see in the media and think that is what is beautiful. That's why advertising and trends are so popular, because they convince people that this is what will make them attractive.

We like to watch Oscar nights and gala nights, and we always pay attention to what the celebrities are wearing. The fashion industry is more than just clothes, accessories and trends. Fashion has huge impact on our society.

"Fashion is the most powerful art there is. It's movement, design, and architecture all in one. It shows the world who we are and who we'd like to be. Just like your scarf suggests that you'd like to sell used cars."
- © Blair Waldorf

High fashion is a form of art. Designers spend a lot of time and creativity on the garments that they show season after season. It is a way to express yourself, you can show the kind of person that you are, who you aren't, what you like or what you don't, all with just a simple accessory or piece. Summing it up, fashion is a daily way to embrace art and express who you are or who you want to be.

If you think about icons from the past - everyone has a very recognizable style and look: Elvis Presley - we all remember his jumpsuit with the big belt and lots of crystals; Marilyn Monroe - platinum blonde with red lipstick; Michael Jackson - his famous hat and diamond glove; Al Capone - well-tailored suit and classic hat; and Audrey Hepburn - with her little black dress. Every star has an image.

Nowadays you can show that you belong to some subculture with the way you dress. Gothic wears all black, the rapper culture demands its own style, hippie and so on. There are readable signs, a specific fashion culture for every class, movement and subculture.

Why do you think that a whole team of fashion consultants, psychologists, advisers, image makers, and makeup artists are working on every single President's look? Because even the tie colour matters, because colour also has a message.

Our look is a message that we are sending to other people about us. Fashion is a way to escape from the boredom of everyday life. It's way to make it more bright and festive. Fashion has no gender and no age.

The psychology of fashion is very deep. Your look, the way you set up your outfit - it is a way to communicate with others. If you want to send a message that you are a professional and take your job seriously, that you are trustful and a go-getter type of person, then you will choose a business style of clothes. I can't imagine the mortgage broker at the bank in jeans, a white tank top, bandana and covered with tattoos. You would not necessarily trust such a person. But who knows, maybe after work that broker does dress exactly like that, but because of his occupation, he is forced to follow the dress code.

You can manipulate people's opinion about you through your clothes, look and image in general. You know who you are, but people will treat you differently when you are in business clothes, or a biker jacket or casual shorts and shirt. That's why dressing properly and according to the weather, occasion, time, and event is key, if you don't want to confuse others. If your goal is to shock people, you can do it through make up, hair and style as well. Try putting on a Halloween costume and make up on a regular day, and you will see the reaction.

Confession #15

When I was in beauty school, as a part of a charity project all the students, along with the teachers, were invited to a Toronto women's shelter. We were doing haircuts for the women who stayed there. There were many women who ran away from abusive relationships or just were not fortunate enough and things were tough for them. So to cheer them up, we were cutting their hair. For us (students), it was great practice.

I remember this woman who was sitting in my chair. She was so depressed, but who would not be? She told me her story.

She immigrated with her husband to Canada a couple of years ago. She had an abusive and very controlling husband and he did not allow her to work here, did not allowed her to dress the way she wanted, and she was not allowed to cut her hair to her taste. Apparently, she was very talented within the IT field. She was so upset because she went on a couple of interviews to find a job, since she left her husband and ended up in the shelter, but no results so far. She was smart, but she looked homeless and her potential bosses did not take her seriously.

I gave her the best haircut that I was able to. Her story touched me so much. The next day, I brought her some clothes and wished her good luck.

A couple of years later, when I was a successful hairstylist in the most prestigious area of Toronto – Yorkville, I had a new client in my chair.

To my big surprise, it was the same woman from the shelter. Now she was a CEO in one of the IT companies. She was successful, happy and looked gorgeous. She told me that way back then she got a job with the new haircut and clothes that I gave her.

Marylin Monroe said, "Give a girl the right shoes, and she can conquer the world." I can say the same thing about the right hairstyle.

Chapter 7
The Truth From Behind The Chair

"There are no facts, only interpretations."

Friedrich Nietzsche

Having worked so many years behind the chair and behind the curtains of the beauty industry, I know all the pros and cons. It might look like a very easy job - beauty, glamour, relaxed chats, friendship - all of it seems to sparkle. But sometimes behind the candelabras, there is a real war. That visual curtain could look pretty, but behind it could be ugly sometimes.

Of course, most of the time, all is well. But let me tell you about the cruelty that I've met behind the scenes.

Assistant

You probably have met that girl who is an assistant in the salon. She makes you coffee, shampoos your hair, sweeps the floor and keeps the salon running smoothly. She does all the dirty work, while trying not to distract the stylist from their main job - to make your hair pretty.

Let me tell you - it's the hardest work. Not many assistants can keep up with all of that and many of them quit their job at this stage.

Sometimes in busy salons, an assistant can provide 20 shampoos in a row without a break. Her back is hurting, her hands are sometimes bleeding from all the chemicals, shampoo and water, but they receive no appreciation. The client wants a massage and an extra rinse and if the client does not get it, then the client is upset. But the stylist works on a schedule, so the shampoo should be done in a certain amount of time. The assistant is caught between two fires: on the one hand, an assistant has to please the client, but on the other hand, she needs to make sure that the client is done on time for the stylist.

Usually, an assistant works hard and for minimum wage. So don't forget to tip your shampoo girl, she really tries her best and works hard.

Another thing is training. Usually after beauty school, the very first job that a person can get is to be an assistant. Since the person is right out of school, no salon will put that person on the floor right away to work with the clients, because of a lack of experience. Obviously that person needs more training - but how does she get that training and experience if she is not allowed to work on the floor and work with clients? That's the question. Usually how it works is the assistant is supervised by a senior stylist, the assistant helps the stylist with the shampoos, sweeping the floor, and getting the coffee/tea for the client. In return, the assistant is trained by the senior stylist, watching how the stylist works and handles the client, among other things. A top salon should send an assistant to take extra courses and training. Sounds good, right? But very often senior stylists just treat the assistant as free help and there is no training in return. I've heard such things as, "Why I should train my competition?" or "It's not my problem". In my opinion, senior stylists should take this more seriously, as you are not raising your competition, but you are raising the next generation of talented stylists for the hairdressing industry. With such a bad attitude, senior stylists with big egos can kill the desire and creativity in the younger generation to continue doing what we do. A tip for a senior stylist - remember that you were in that position too. Don't try to make it harder. Be helpful and become a teacher, mentor and coach for your assistant, as it is a big honour to be able to train somebody younger. It means you are experienced, trustful and wise, if the salon lets you train somebody. Take this as a privilege and recognition of your status, experience and talent.

Also, the salon should legally register the student as an apprentice in the salon. After about a year, a student can go and take a test to get a hairdressing license to become a registered hairstylist. It's a lot of pressure on a young inexperienced stylist-to-be.

Confession #16

Her name is Tasha. She finished beauty school 3 years ago. She was working at a great salon with a big name. After working there nearly

2 years, Tasha asked the owner about working on the floor, and whether or not she was due to take the exam to get her license. The owner told her that she was not trained enough yet, so she must keep assisting. Tasha was disappointed and frustrated. She had already been assisting more than 2 years and never received any training. Basically, she was used as cheap help and never received anything in return, which was promised before she started her job. So she quit and went to another salon to start all over again.

Tasha was one of the best students in the school. She is passionate about hair, plus she is honest, hard-working and very talented.

The new salon promised her the legal registration as an apprentice and training. She start working again – cleaning the salon, doing laundry, folding the towels, sweeping the floor, and shampooing the clients' hair. She worked hard. Six months later, she asked about being trained by a senior stylist and when she could go to take her exam. The manager told Tasha that she does her job so well that they don't want to promote her to become a junior stylist. They will be not able to find a replacement, because she did her job so well.

Tasha was in shock. It meant that she wasted 3 years of her life on cleaning and did not come any closer to her dream of becoming a hairstylist, even though she has a beauty school diploma.

She went to work at a construction company, as she had no faith in the beauty industry any more. After half a year, she called me and asked for help. She told me that her dream was to be a hairstylist, that construction was not for her. She wanted to try one more time, but she was afraid that she would be betrayed again.

I helped her. She is a very hard working person, very dedicated to her work and very talented. It was a big loss for the salons who let her go, as she was a great assistant, but now she is a brilliant stylist who is fully booked two weeks ahead.

As a business owner, always look for the potential of your workers. As a person, never use people, as what you put out into the world - that is what you get back. Karma, you know.

I don't know why the word "hairstylist" has such a powerful impact on people. For example, when I am with new company, at a bar, at a restaurant - wherever I meet new people, usually when people hear my occupation, hairstylist, right away they start sharing their hair problems. – "Oh, my hair is so greasy, what can I do?" – "I have dandruff - what is the solution?" Usually I say, "Here is my business card, please make an appointment and let's see what can be done." Very often people don't get it and still continue to show me their hair, scalp and tell me stories. They don't understand - when I am eating or not working, I don't want to see your re-growth, the pimples on your scalp, or other issues. It's my work, so let's keep it professional.

If I was a dentist or gynecologist – would you still show me your wide open mouth in the bar, or even worse?

Confession #17

It happened to me a couple of years ago. I was having my lunch at one of the local restaurants. Sitting next to me was a woman whom I had seen many times, as she was working in one of the offices above the salon. We often saw each other, but never really were introduced to each other. Since we were both eating next to each other and recognized each other, we started chatting. She told me that she is a mother of two, working in the office above the salon. As soon as I told her that I am a hairstylist, she winked at me and told me that she had something to show me.

She slid her hand in her purse and extracted a little plastic bag, like a Ziploc.

Then she started smiling and pulled out three locks of hair, putting them right on the dinner table, along with a couple of small teeth. I froze, as I did not expect that. I lost my appetite right away.

She told me that two of the locks of hair belonged to her children, and the other one was from a very dear person, her Grandmother, who had passed away. The teeth were her children's calf teeth. I told her that it was disgusting to show such things while a person is eating.

Confessions of the Hairstylist

She called me a heartless bitch, as in her opinion it was very cute and carried a lot of memories for her. She believed that because I worked with hair all the time, I should be used to seeing hair.

Sometimes personal things are called personal for a reason. What looks cute to you can be unacceptable for others. It's hygiene and morality at the end, and sometimes just plain eating etiquette.

You probably have noticed that almost all hairstylists wear black. Sometimes it's even funny, when I am at a hair seminar or hair show and the most creative, vibrant, and eccentric people on the planet wear black. It looks like a sea of black. After all these years, I've noticed that most of my wardrobe consists of black pieces. Why is it that way?

There are a couple of reasons.

Black is a very strong colour. It's a safe colour, very slimming and brings some mystery, which is nice, because hairstylists are hair magicians.

Also, I think it's because black is a lot cleaner, crisper and a professional looking colour, rather than tank tops, jeans and multicoloured clothing.

A lot of salons have a dress code and black is suitable for everyone. You can add some coloured earrings, a scarf or necklaces to make it look less boring. Black emphasizes nice make up, and of course, sharp hair, which is very important; as a hairstylist's look and hair is the best business advertising.

Also when you wear black, you are showing that the only superstar in the salon is the client in your chair. Your client should shine, not you. You are a professional licensed hair magician who can make it happen. It's not about the stylist, it's about the client.

We work with hair colours and bleach all the time, so black is a very handy colour.

When we splash hair colour on it, you can't tell easily. Hair colour is not visible on the black and you can touch up bleach spots with a black marker.

Also imagine - standing behind a client whom you have just coloured saying, "What an amazing shade of red!" and you, in contrast, are wearing a TURQUOISE top. How does that look in the mirror? It's going to look like a mess, plus your clothes are ruined, and that means you need to spend more to buy something new.

Another thing - jealousy wars between the stylists. Usually a manager or owner of the salon will not let that happen, but sometimes it does occur. There are good and bad people among hairstylists, as well as in any other industry. I am talking about their personalities. Some people don't want to grow professionally, and as a result, they are not that busy. That means they are making less money. Instead of focusing on professional growth, they try to destroy the business of their colleagues. It's called envy. And it could be brutal. Sometimes they will steal the cards with a client's formula and the other stylist needs to figure out the formula once again. But they may not use what was adjusted for the client already, or mix tubes with colours in different packs, as all the colour tubes go by number according to a paper pack. So the other stylist thinks she has the right formula, but ends up losing the client. Sometimes they steal or hide your tools and equipment. Every hairstylist will tell you that tools are an extension of the hands and cost lots of money.

Usually those trouble-makers are fired immediately, but they can cause a lot of damage to the salon, its reputation and everyone's money in the meantime.

How should you behave when a client and stylist clash?

Although this may not be easy for either the client or the stylist to hear, the truth is that both can have objectives or moods that simply clash. Maybe not always, but from time to time, tension can develop, and the goal is to defuse it—or to know when you have a mismatch and need to move on to someone else.

Ask your friends or salon employees who don't do hair and you'll often hear that stylists can be a sensitive, tricky group of artists. Oftentimes, ego gets in the way of reason, but there absolutely are stylists out there who are exceedingly talented, yet humble.

Stylists often will ask for your feedback, but then seem to ignore or disregard everything you say. However, you also must keep in mind that lots of clients want haircuts that won't work for their hair type, or they have completely unrealistic expectations about what's possible with their hair. A stylist must deal with such situations delicately; some are true pros at this, while others don't know how to tell a client that his or her hair wish is unrealistic or impossible to achieve, which doesn't insure either party will be satisfied with the result.

Stylists have a difficult job. Most are on their feet all day long, while trying to make their clients look great, even if they have wispy, seriously damaged, over-dyed, or difficult-to-manage hair. As clients, we need to understand that hairstylists, even the incredibly talented ones, aren't miracle workers. If we show up with seriously damaged hair, we cannot expect to walk out looking like we're ready to star in a shampoo ad!

Salon Etiquette for a Stylist

1. **Don't be late.** Always find a way to inform your client when you are running late or are overbooked. Respect the other person's time. It is not nice to have your client sitting in the waiting area wondering what happened. If you're running behind longer than

half an hour, offer to reschedule the appointment at a discounted rate and go the extra mile by offering extra services for free, such as a deep conditioning treatment or blow out. Respect your client's time.

2. **Be patient and kind.** Not everyone knows the difference between highlights and low lights, but every single client wants to have a great hair cut or colour. Take your time and explain the difference, even using visual images from your iPad, phone or magazine. Explain everything. Always ask your client if they have any questions about what you are going to do, how to maintain it at home, and if they do, answer in full.

3. **Be clear about the costs.** Some clients don't do research on the prices of your services. It is your responsibility to inform the client how much it will cost at the end. You are the one who must be up front about what everything is going to cost. There is a big difference between a roots touch up and a colour correction. Each service has a price and always clarify that to your client before you start the service. It is very uncomfortable for both when at the end the client is shocked by the bill.

4. **Honesty is the best policy, up to a point.** Listen to your client. Don't try to impress with your creativity. Be patient and listen. If the client has unrealistic expectations, explain why it cannot be achieved on this service or in general. Never make a client feel

insecure. With a kind smile and tone of voice, offer an alternative or explain the whole process. Instead of a flat-out "no"—kindly explain.

5. **Don't expect tips.** I would say don't expect tips at all. Clients are paying for the service as it is priced, so do your best to meet the client's expectations. In Asia, for example, tips for a hairstylist are humiliating, as it means that you are in a lower position, but you are not. You are a professional and need to do your job accordingly. Tips are always something extra, not a must. People show their appreciation with their tips. The motto is: Expect the cost of the service, but work for the tip.

6. **No cell phones on the salon floor!** It is disrespectful and rude when your clients wait, while you check your cell phone, email, respond to a text message, or "Like" a post on Facebook or Instagram. When you're on the salon floor, you're on the job. Your superstar is right in your chair and all your attention should be focused on your client and your job, not on your cell phone.

7. **Keep the conversation easy, pleasant and professional.** Never talk about religion, money, sex, romance, or even politics. Don't gossip about the salon, clients and coworkers. It is a very intimate business, because you are working one-on-one. So it could be tempting to share some details about your personal life for an opinion on these off-limit topics, but don't do it. Whatever you

do, be mindful not to put the client in the crossfire of the details. Don't make your client feel uncomfortable. Focus on your client's hairdo.

8. **Always look and act professional**ly. Dress for success and always care about the client.

Salon Etiquette for the Client

1. **Don't be late.** When you are late by a couple minutes or so, expect to have a shorter service or no service at all and to be rescheduled. Sometimes it does happen that you will be late, but take responsibility for it. Always call and let the salon know that you are going to be late. You are not running behind on just your schedule, but you are making your stylist run behind on her schedule too. If your stylist is late working with you, it means she would be late to start on another client. Every service - cut, colour or blowout - has its own time, so if you are late, you need to be ready to be rushed through or rescheduled. Better to be on time or even a couple of minutes early.

2. **Be prepared and bring pictures of the haircuts, styles or colour you love.** Come ready and have some saved or printed pictures of the hairdo that you love. Discuss with your stylist what you have in mind, but be prepared to accept it if the answer is no. Sometimes the desired style just simply does not work realistically

with your hair. Stylists will offer an alternative style or clearly explain why it is not possible to achieve. As I say: "I only have shears, not magic dust."

3. **Inform the stylist how much time you spend on styling your hair every day.** If you are not ready to spend a couple of minutes on styling – don't ask for a complicated cut, just tell the stylist that you are looking for a wash and go style. Just be honest. A great cut is only the half way point; the other half is how you maintain your style at home.

4. **Know beforehand the price for the services you're asking for.** As a client, it's your responsibility to find out what your stylist is charging, and the services that you are requesting from them. It is a very unpleasant "surprise", when after everything is done, to be shocked with the bill. Visit the salon's website or ask over the phone, but be very clear on the prices according to the service. Usually salons offer a free consultation, so book one, explain your problem, ask for the price and then book the appointment.

5. **Don't be too shy to speak up and please do it in a kind manner.** The best way to avoid a misunderstanding is to clear up all the details before the service begins. As the client, you can expect a high level of customer service, but it's also your responsibility to be gracious in return. Don't change your mind numerous times during the service. When it's done, then it's done. Trust me, a

stylist knows when a client is being unreasonably difficult or mean. Stylists can always fire you as a client, so you don't need to be a drama queen!

6. **If a stylist meets your expectations and you are happy - TIP!** A gratuity usually is 10–20% of the service. When you are buying products on top of that, tip on amount of your service, not the bill in total. Believe me, a stylist has a good memory for the clients who tip well. So next time you try to make an appointment at the last minute or if you need to be squeezed in, the stylist will choose you.

7. **Don't try to become your stylist's BFF (best friend forever).** Stylists are working one-on-one with the client, so it is very intimate. If you see your stylist on a regular basis, the chances are high that you will share some personal information. That does not mean that the stylist is your friend outside of the salon. Keep it professional. In the salon, it is all about the hair.

8. **Use your cell phone only in an emergency.** Even if you don't want to chat with your stylist, it's rude to text, be emailing on your phone or to be making calls. You might be in the way of the stylist's work. Don't do it, as it will be uncomfortable for both of you. Sooner or later that call will end, and you can't blame the stylist for the so-so work that results.

When Things Go Wrong (What the Hell happened to My Hair?)

Even the best stylists are human beings and they have bad days. Sometimes even the greatest stylist can make a mistake. How do you handle that?

Stylists don't argue, even if they disagree. They listen to the client, apologize truly, and offer to fix it as soon as possible.

- Stylists understand that the most important thing is their client, so no one needs to feel traumatized. Nobody should be shocked or insulted. Pretty much every hair mistake or disaster can be fixed. At the end of the day, it is only hair.

- It's in the stylist's best interest to keep you as a long-term client. So a stylist will offer her best option to fix the problem or recommend someone who can.

But what if it happens when you are the client and you hate how your hair turned out? Don't scream and break down in tears. That's not the best way. All you need to do is speak up right then and there, but in a constructive and kind manner as is possible (even if you're freaking out inside). So my advice is:

- First of all, don't be shy and tell your stylist or front desk girl that you're unhappy with how your hair turned out.

- Be as specific as possible. Is it way too short or long, too blonde or red? Tell them exactly what you don't like about your hairdo. Ask what can be done and when.

- It is OK if you don't pay for the service until it is done to your satisfaction. Whether fixed on the same day, or at a later date that's convenient for both you and your stylist, do not pay for a salon service if you're unhappy with the results. If the salon asks you for the payment, be sure you have written confirmation that the cost to fix the problem will be zero, in other words, free.

- Next time be sure to discuss with your stylist any concerns you have about how your hair might have turned out. Perhaps the problem was due to the dye being left on too long, so the timing needs to be adjusted, or maybe you forgot to tell your stylist you had coloured your hair with henna (colour turns out differently on previously dyed hair versus virgin hair). Make sure you don't hide any information that can cause a problem, and thus prevent it from happening in future.

Tips

Finding a good stylist can be very challenging. So when you find the perfect match, you have to be good to keep them happy—and when it comes to keeping your hairstylist happy, it is important to know the expectations for tipping. So how do you tip? Here are some recommendations for tips that are almost universal.

If you're happy with your hair, **you should tip your stylist 15% to 20% of your total service.** An easy way to calculate this is figure of 10% (move the decimal point over one to the left), then add half the amount of that figure for a 15% total tip. So, a $50.00 bill becomes $7.50 ($5 + $2.50). Calculate a 20% tip by multiplying the 10% (decimal point to the left) by two.

- **If more than one person was involved in creating your style, tip them too.** If your stylist had an assistant (shampooing, blow-drying or bringing you something to drink), consider tipping them $5 to $10, depending how much they catered to your needs.

- **If the owner of the salon is your stylist, you should still tip them.** You may think the old fashion way of not tipping the salon owner is still true, but overwhelmingly, we found this not the case. Whether your hairstylist is the salon owner or not, tipping 15% to 20% is still a good way to show your appreciation.

- **During the holidays, tip more to your stylist.** Tip a little more than usual on holidays! Does not matter how long you have been visiting your stylist (and, of course, how much your services cost per visit), consider $20 to $75 more during the holiday season or a good bottle of champagne.

The Bottom Line is..

To a client, the salon environment (especially a new salon) can seem intimidating. The tips above will help you feel more in control and capable of handling the mix ups, but more often, they will keep your talented stylist happy and prolong the productive relationship between you and your stylist.

As a stylist, you're in a unique position to make your clients look and feel like a million bucks. They're trusting (and paying) you to make them look good, and they deserve your full attention and the full extent of your talents. Keeping and maintaining a positive experience for every client will reward you in full, both personally and professionally.

Chapter 8
Your Look Is Your Self-Esteem's Reflection

"Dress, hairstyles and makeup are the most obvious signs of self-affirmation. If fashion governs personal appearance to such an extent, it is because fashion is a privileged way of expressing the uniqueness of individuals."

Gilles Lipovetsky,

The Empire of Fashion: Dressing Modern Democracy,

Princeton: Princeton University Press, 1994

Women also change with the men they are around. A woman has a more flexible personality and she will fit herself to the man. Have you ever asked yourself why the same woman acts differently with different men? That is because she does not like emptiness. She is filling the emptiness. If a man is too feminine, she will act way too masculine. If a man is not mature, she will play the "mama" role and so on.

This game is very dangerous. A woman can lose herself in this game. She can lose her personality. Don't blame the woman for that. It is just because of our nature. A woman's nature is a process. Man's nature is the result.

Always be true to yourself!

The way we dress is the way that we want other people to understand us. It is a different way of communication with the world.

When we want to show our best, then we dress accordingly. When we want to hide, then we dress very casually. This is as if you are trying to say, "I am invisible. Don't bug me."

Confession #18
This lady is a professional mistress. Let's put aside the moral aspect of it for a moment. This is what she says about her line of work.

"I have this business just because women let me. Women think if they are in relationships or married, then they cannot look after themselves. How many of you put on makeup for your man or dress nicely at home? She thinks if she has this man, then he will never leave her. But the truth is when you just started dating, you always tried to look nice for him and that is a part of why he was after you. When a child is born, then a woman usually put the kids in first place and a man feels lonely. Also, he feels that you kind of lied to him. He married a pretty woman, but now she is different with that dirty hair bun and old yoga pants, no more skirts, dresses, and makeup. Women usually destroy this by themselves, that's why I am busy. A man comes to me because he wants, for a couple of hours, to just be surrounded by beauty. I put a lot of effort into my look. Manicure, pedicure, hair, makeup,

cosmetologist, and nice lingerie. Another thing is they stop talking to their men about anything except diapers, what to cook for dinner, the groceries and mundane household stuff. A man also needs romance and that is what I am giving to men. Women are losing their identity with this everyday life of kids and work. They forget that they are Queens. She is the whole Universe to her man, so make it beautiful."

No two women look the same. Every woman has her own style and taste. The polished look is complete with good grooming. It does not matter how expensive your dress is if your body smells or your nail polish is chipped. Without good grooming, you are destroying your whole look. There are some self-grooming tips that everyone should follow.

The Grooming Guide

Cleanliness
It is very important to shower regularly. It is not pleasant to smell unwashed body odor and no fragrance can hide it. Also, some places are fragrance-free, so the smell of a freshly washed body is a must.

Choose a body wash to your taste and enjoy. To make it more relaxing, you can take a bath with lighted candles and your favourite bubble bath or oils. It will not only benefit your body, but also your mood.

I like to take a bath in the morning instead of a shower. Time wise, it's only a couple of minutes longer, but it is my way of meditating and concentrating on the good things that the coming day will bring to me.

Skin

The basis and the foundation for every woman's beauty is her healthy and glowing skin.

Don't forget to wash your face every morning and every evening. Using toner and your moisturizer are a must. In the long run, it will pay you back, so invest in good products according to your skin type.

Skin masks and scrubs can help you to remove the dead skin layer and put beneficial ingredients in your skin at a deeper layer. The best way to do it is to have it done professionally with a licensed cosmetologist, but there are many products designed for home use. Rest and enough sleep is very important, as this is the time when your skin is rejuvenated. No makeup and no products can hide tiredness. Also, don't underestimate the benefits that come from a massage. It helps to relax the muscles and keep your skin toned and firm.

Drink plenty of water, as hydration is the key. Just love your skin and take care of it. It will pay you back with a healthy glow and long lasting youthful look.

Hair

Your hair is your crown that you cannot take off, so wear it proudly. Your hair is beautiful when it is shaped accordingly to your facial features, when it is cut well and when the hair colour compliments your complexion and eye colour. To keep your hair healthy, shiny and moisturized, wash it when it is dirty. No need to wash it every day, especially if your hair is dry. In that case, you are removing natural oils and moisture from your hair. The main rule for how often to wash your hair is to only wash it when it is dirty. Use shampoo, conditioner, hair masks and oil according to your hair type. It is best to ask your hair stylist what works best for you. Never go over due with your hair colour. Learn how to style your hair at home. Wearing your hair every day in a ponytail or bun is not a style. Ask your hairstylist how you can maintain your cut and colour at home.

To look expensive with your hair cut, don't choose anything over the top. Go with a simple, elegant but stylish cut. Forget about those crazy layered cuts or the cuts that require a lot of maintenance, unless you are going for blow dries weekly. The same with your hair colour. Don't go crazy on the colours. I prefer to choose something natural looking, like soft ombre or sun-kissed looks. Remember that harsh streak highlights were left in the 90's. Choose something subtler that compliments you.

Your hair products, like shampoo, oils, tools, and brushes, are a little luxury that you are bringing to your everyday life. You don't need to buy a Gucci suit but you can wear a Gucci fragrance and that is going to upgrade you to that luxury mood. Invest in a good hair dryer, heated tools and brushes. Master your skills and you will do your hair like a pro. Remember cheap hair looks frizzy; too much teasing will result in split ends, greasy roots, and unmanageable layers; strong odors can come from dry shampoo; and luxury hair looks shiny with soft texture and touchable with volume and smooth texture.

Nails

Hands are your business card. A manicure is a little detail that gives you that polished luxury look. Keep your hands clean with a regular manicure and keep them well moisturized. Don't forget to wear gloves while you are gardening or doing dishes. That's going to protect your skin and also make your nail polish last longer. Always have polish remover at home in case your nails are chipped, so you can quickly remove it by yourself. It is better to go with naked nails, then with chipped nails.

Makeup

Makeup can bring that glamorous, stylish and finished look. Why has nude makeup remained so popular over the decades? It's because it suits everyone, while still looking stylish and elegant. There is nothing uglier than running foundation, smudging mascara, bleeding lips or lipstick on your teeth. Always keep lip balm with you. Moisturized plump lips always look better than half eaten bright lipstick. For eye shadows, choose nude colours or colours that compliment your eye colour versus the latest trends that you see on celebrities. Remember that a whole team of stylists and makeup artists are working on one look for that celebrity. Not every experiment can go well when you do it yourself. Don't forget to remove your makeup before you go to bed to give your skin some rest.

Perfume

Odor has a big impact on the way people perceive you. Have you ever been in a situation where you don't like a person's perfume and you don't want to continue talking to them? Never be cheap with your perfume. Don't buy fake cheap knock offs, as it's not going to last or it's not going to smell the same. Your perfume should be your signature smell, so choose it wisely. Remember there are people who are very sensitive to smells, so an elegant, classic fragrance will be your best choice. Don't mix different perfumes together, since they can create an unpleasant smell. Another thing is to try to choose your body care products with a soft smell or perfume free, because a different smell from your body lotion or hand cream can be in conflict with your perfume.

Also, remember that a little goes a long way, so there is no need to overdo the application of your perfume.

Final Touches

Remember to shape your eyebrows. Keep your skin hair free, especially on the legs and under arms. Don't forget the little details, like the hair above your upper lip. Then have gum or breath freshener wherever you go. Play with accessories. Love yourself.

Ask yourself these questions:

1. Do my clothes suit my figure and personality?
2. Am I standing out from the crowd in a positive way or do I look invisible in the sea of sameness?
3. Am I a fashion victim who buys every latest trend in clothes?
4. What do I prefer, quality or quantity?
5. Do I know what colours suit me the best?
6. Am I using jewelry and accessories?
7. Am I always dressed according to the weather, time, event, and occasion?
8. Do I plan my outfit ahead of time?
9. Do I look after my clothes and shoes? Am I always putting away my shoes clean and polished, ready to wear for the next time?

The answer should be "Yes!".

Think about this and figure out who you are and what works the best for you.

Jean-Paul Gautier said, "Elegance is a question of personality more than one's clothing."

Looking good at all times is a combination of little things put together and creating that final complex look that is called your personal style.

The most important thing at all times is your self-esteem. You need to love yourself and respect yourself first, before expecting it from others.

Chapter 9
Who I Am And How I Became A Hairstylist

"But eyes are blind. You have to look with the heart."
Antoine de Saint Exupery "Little Prince"

My name is Anastasia. I am a hairstylist and I am proud of it.

What made me choose this profession and did I always know that I would be a hairdresser?

Have you thought about why people all over the world admire Mona Lisa's smile by Leonardo da Vinci? What did Bach or Beethoven want to express through their divine music? Can you see the story behind every architectural masterpiece? I am excited to watch ballet, listen to opera or read a book. I have tears flowing from Van Gogh paintings or even a good movie. Have you ever thought what the world of art actually is?

I know this is not easy. I had a long road to this profession. I went from the distrust of my relatives and friends who believed that I was ruining my life and that I would never make enough money working in the service industry. But what can be better than to serve people on an everyday basis and meet their needs? I think it's the greatest source of happiness and the purpose of my life.

I think they don't understand that this is a big part of my life, something that lives inside me and needs to be expressed. That it's my art, my way to make this world beautiful. If you at least once see the thankful eyes of your client, then you will understand that you cannot circumvent the trust you have been given. If you have the need to make people happy, beautiful and confident, to introduce them to the divine world of art, then you will feel respect for this profession.

I want to show this beautiful world to every single client in the salon, bring the art into their everyday life and help them improve their lives, as we all know that your look is a reflection of your self-esteem.

I want every woman to feel the need to come to the salon, relax, trust their hairdresser and touch the beauty through her hairstyle. It's so important.

At the end of the day, I could be really tired, but I know for sure that I did not waste my time, my day, and my life. As long as I am able to help people feel more beautiful, more confident and important, I know that I am doing everything right.

I was born in Ukraine (in a small town in the West), a wonderful European country with a picturesque nature and kind people. I was lucky to be born into a loving and caring artistic family.

Everything starts with my grandmother. She did not have a proper school education, but intuitively she felt that beauty was very important in her life. She did not have money to buy nice and fashionable clothes, so she learned how to sew. She studied at the best modiste at that time in our region. Since that time, my grandmother always looks fabulous. Even now at 85 years old, she still has the patience and fantasy to fix herself a new dress or suit. That's why my Mom was raised with an appreciation of fashion, beauty and art. My mother is a teacher of literature and a writer. She is the one who opened me up to the magical world of books. My father is a teacher of music and a sound director. He is the one who introduced me to the world of music. My father's parents are also very artistic and creative. My grandfather was a painter and my grandmother is an embroiderer. So art is in my blood. I have that intuitive understanding and appreciation for beauty and I see it everywhere and in everybody. I deeply and truly believe that every single one of us is unique and beautiful in his/her own way. And when I talk about beauty, it is not only about the external things. Beauty comes from inside. One of the most beautiful and famous women on the earth, Audrey Hepburn, said, "For beautiful eyes, look for the good in others; for beautiful lips, speak only words of kindness; and for poise, walk with the knowledge that you are never alone." I am trying to say that beauty is not about just a pretty face. It is about having a pretty mind, a pretty heart, and a pretty soul.

At the age of 7, I went to art school. I studied painting, sculpture, music, and architecture. At that time, I started playing violin. That's how I know, understand and adore classical music, actually any kind or style of music. I was discovering the magical world of art in different forms - music, ballet, opera, dance, and literature, and I fell in love with it. I always wanted to find a way to express my creativity and I've found one - hairdressing.

My very first clients were my younger sister and my dog Tomik. My poor sister always had a short haircut during her childhood, that's why she adores her long hair now. All the trouble usually would start with the phrase, "Hey, sister, I have an idea for your new cut. Do you want to look cool?" Of course, what can you do when you are 10 years old? Usually we ended up at the salon with professional help. Thank God, one of my Mom's friends was a hairdresser. I remember when we all would go to her salon - it was a magical world for me. The smells of hairspray, perms, shampoo and the sound of the scissors just transferred me to another world or even more - to another galaxy.

While waiting for my sister's hair to grow back, I had my dog, of course, not to mention my dolls. My lovely pet was my first client for really short cuts, hair tattooing and more. Let me tell you, on my street I had the most fashionable dog: sometimes with a Leo cut - you know, when only the mane and end of the tail are left unshaved or other crazy "hair-dos".

After finishing high school with really great marks, it was a time to decide what I wanted to study and what I wanted to make as my profession.

Of course, my passion was hairdressing. So when I told my parents that I was going to hairdressing school, they screamed, "Are you nuts? Girl, choose a real profession and a normal future." So it was a deal - first I needed to finish University and then I could do whatever I wanted. So I entered Kyiv National Linguistic University and after 5 years I successfully finished it. Was that time a waste? Absolutely NOT. The most important things were that I got my teacher's diploma, I learned how to organize my time, learned new skills, and met a lot of people. I moved to another city, so I also learned how to live on my own and be responsible for the choices I had made. At University, I learned the most important thing - how to get things done, or if you can't do something - find a way and have it done anyway. Basically, I went from a taker to a go-getter person. That was the biggest lesson of my life. Of course, during those 5 years, I was always doing hair on the side. It was my hobby - to create an updo for my roommate when she was going on her first date, or colour somebody's hair for disco night.

After University, I decided to stay in the capital of Ukraine, the most beautiful city in the world - Kyiv. Why? Simply put, there were more job opportunities for me.

There is nothing more constant than temporary things. I decided to find a job to be able to pay for my hairdressing school. Since I had my diploma as a teacher - I was hired by a school. I loved my job, but I did not get any satisfaction from what I was doing. I felt that I was missing something in my life.

After two years of teaching, I decided to try a different industry and went to the corporate world. I was good at what I did, but I was not happy. If you are a working person and not at your own place - you would understand: I was waiting for Fridays because it meant that the work week was over. Mondays always were the hardest days as the whole week was ahead of me. When you are dealing with a job that you don't like every day, month after month, you become unhappy about your life in general. It is understandable as a third of my life was spent on a job that I didn't like and it became even worse, to the point that I start hating it.

I realized that I didn't want to live like that anymore. I didn't want to go to work doing something I didn't like, to make money just to buy gadgets, stuff or clothes to impress people that I did not even care about, just to create that illusion of a successful young professional person. The more materialistic stuff I had - the more I needed, as now

I needed a bigger apartment to have space for all my stuff, more money to upgrade whatever I had to a better or newer version - that way was a way to nowhere. I tried to fill the emptiness inside my soul with stuff that I could buy. I realized that something was missing in my life, something was wrong, and it was not working. I didn't want to live like that anymore. I needed changes. I needed dramatic changes. Sometimes you need to take a step back, and go back to your source to see the bigger picture and realize where you want to go now with your life.

For me, such a step back or break was a trip to Canada. It was my vacation time and I always had a dream - to see Niagara Falls. So I bought a ticket and went.

Twenty-four hours after I left Ukraine, I was standing in front of Niagara Falls. I was watching that enormous amount of water falling every second, felt the spray, that smell and heard that roar and power of nature and I felt happy, truly happy. I will always remember that amazing feeling when my dream came true. Niagara Falls was so impossible for that little girl from the small town in the West of Ukraine and there I was, standing just in front of it and with all my senses engaged, experiencing my dream. Since then when I have a down moment, I just pull out of the closets of my memory that feeling and it gives me inspiration and a belief that everything is possible, and the sky is the limit.

No more experiments with my life. I knew what I wanted to do. I knew what I enjoyed doing and always knew. It was hairdressing. I clearly understood that I needed to finish hairdressing school to get a license and be able to do what I really loved. I told myself that it's going to be in Canada. I had already gone out of my comfort zone. The decision had been made. Now it left only the technical details - study permission, papers, school and everything that went with an international move.

After spending some time in Niagara Falls, I moved to Toronto. I called my family and told them that I was staying in Canada to do my dream work - hairdressing. What a relief I felt when I called my boss and told him that he could fire me - I didn't care, I was not coming back. A new chapter of my life was just about to begin.

I went to one of the most prestigious hairdressing schools in Toronto, set up a meeting with the director and told him, "Ok, what kind of papers should I fill out, as I have decided to become one of your students." You should have seen his face. He was shocked by my confidence and my impudence. Obviously, this is not how things work in Canada. I was told that first I needed to pass the exams and depending on my score, they would let me know if I qualified. Sure enough, I passed my tests successfully and I became a proud student of Marvel School. I knew that now nothing could stop me from achieving my dream.

I became one of the best students. I loved the stuff that I was learning. I was listening to every word that the teacher was saying and finally everything felt right in my life. I was at the right place at the right time. Everything that I was doing as a hobby for years was now filled with professional education, knowledge and practice.

I was so inspired, happy and I couldn't get enough. I started doing hair for photo-shoots on the side for other students, photographers or clothing designers. I discovered hair competitions. I wanted to see what other hairstylists could do and show off my work as well. In 2012, I became a finalist of the most prestigious competitions in Canada in the student category. Can you imagine? I became one of the top five student-hairstylists from all over Canada. I was in heaven.

That is how it works sometime. You need to lose your comfortable life in order to receive your dream life, get out of your comfort zone, do things that you have never done before, take risks, take responsibility and trust the Universe. That is what worked for me.

During my training, I was enjoying my life. I was traveling by car around Canada. I was discovering this country and falling in love with it more and more. I went by car all the way East. I saw the picturesque beauty of the nature of Quebec, peaceful life in Nova Scotia, great roads in New Brunswick, traditions of the natives in Nunavut, the best lobster dishes in local private owned restaurants in Prince Edward Island, and of course, breathtaking views of the Atlantic Ocean on Newfoundland coast.

I got my scuba-diving license as well. Now I was able to enjoy Canada and the world in general, not only on the surface, but underwater as well. Since then, I have gotten a lot of my inspiration during my dives. This is a different world, an undiscovered world with different inhabitants, nature, character and with its own rules. I love those moments when you pass the first 5-7 meters deep into the water and all that you see is so unusual. You focus on your breathing, you still see the sunlight through the depth of water but it's different, it's like you never saw the Sun from that view and perspective, you see the bottom of the body of water. I feel like I am on different planet, like I am in space or even in a different Galaxy. It's one of my ways to meditate.

Needless to say, I've successfully finished school and became a proud owner of a Diploma in hairstyling.

Of course to get your license, you need to complete a certain amount of training hours, and I was eager to start. The question was - when and where? I ended up in a salon in the most prestigious part of Toronto - Yorkville. I could not believe that this was my life now. What a difference compared to the life that I had only 1 year ago!

After a couple years, I became a salon owner. I opened my own shop exclusively for women. Why women exclusively? There are many unisex salons around, so everyone can choose a place for their needs, budget and comfort. I wanted to create that relaxing comfortable atmosphere for my clients, a place where they can come, relax, enjoy a good cup of freshly made coffee, feel comfortable during the process, chat about the latest trends and more. So I created a kind of women's beauty club. I stand very strong for womanhood. During the last couple of years, I was working with women on a daily basis, since my clientele was mostly women. I witnessed happiness, divorces, newborn babies, deaths of loved ones, job losses, abusive boyfriends/husbands and romantic relationships with a nice wedding at the end. On the other hand, there was also menopause, hot flashes and other joys of aging. Every lady had a story, and as I am a woman myself, I understand that need sometimes to discuss these things or situations with another woman. I know it sounds strange but people in the hairdresser's chair talk a lot. Sometimes sharing too many details that I should not know or don't want to know. For example, I had one client in my chair who shared some very intimate information. During her hair service, she was describing how hot her boyfriend was, what he liked in bed, what he does to her intimately and even imitated his moaning during the process and the funny face he makes when he climaxes. Why do I need to know that? The next time he came to the salon to pick up my client, the only thing that I could imagine was his funny face and the strange noises that he makes. Ladies, please be mindful when you are sharing personal information. Hairstylists are not your best friends with whom you can share all those details. Hairstylists are individuals whom you hire to make you look your best. I am sure you would not share such information with your dentist or mechanic, so please don't do it with your hairstylist, cosmetologist or beauty consultant. I am one of those stylists who respects my client's privacy. I never share any personal information about my clients. My clients know it and we have built that trust over the years. But let me tell you that in this industry not everyone is like me. I witnessed many times when a hairstylist played it cool with you and a couple of minutes later was discussing your secrets in the salon staff room with their colleagues and giggling. It's not ethical, I know, but don't forget - it's the human factor. You never know who you are dealing with. So it's better to keep your personal things to yourself.

I wanted to create a place where busy Moms can come and have that two hours of escape from their routine, or a business woman can focus and work on her laptop while her hair colour is processing and that concept of women exclusively, no men, no kids, works great in my case.

Of course, I miss my family and my friends who stayed back home, but I was happy that I did make that move and turned my life into something amazing. My sister got married, my parents have an established life, so I knew they were not going to move here. Thank God, it's the 21st century and we have all these technologies to keep in touch with. I Skype or Facetime my family all the time, so it feels as though we are close and just live in different cities, not that there is an ocean between us. How often do you meet with your family members who live in a different city or even the same city? I bet it's like the usual things - Christmas, family reunions and a couple other holidays. So I fly back every New Year or Christmas, and my Mom visits me at other times. It's not like it was in the 19th century. I cannot even imagine how different things were back then. For example, you write a letter (hey, not an email), an actual letter, and send it by sea. Until it gets to the person, a couple of months have already come and gone. Then the person writes a reply and you are lucky if that happens right away, then the same couple of months on the way back. If you are lucky enough that your letter was not lost during the transportation process, you will receive an answer. So to send a letter and to receive a note back, you need to wait around half a year? No, thanks. I would rather use Viber or something like that and not only hear, but SEE my beloved ones right away, right this moment.

Life really has a sense of humor. I truly believe what is meant to be will be. But also don't forget that actions are a must. I am not teaching you how to live and not saying that I am right or my way is the only way. I am speaking from my experience. I made that extra loop in my life journey. Do I regret it? No! Who knows if I would have become a hairstylist right after high school? Maybe I would have quickly become disappointed in this industry, because it's a really tough industry even though it looks so glamorous and beautiful from the outside. Maybe I would not be so grateful for my talent and passion, because I would not know what it means to waste your time and life on things that you don't like. As a result, I know what it is like to suffer from depression, how it is to spend those endless hours, days, weeks, and months doing the things that you don't like and don't care about. Yes, I needed money to live on, but those words like joy, happiness, and purpose of life were not related to me. I am so happy that at the end I did not struggle with my passion and just went with the flow. Now I can say I am truly deeply happy. I do what I love, I lose track of time when I am working, as I am happy and delighted with what I do. I can't wait until morning and I am jumping out of bed as I am excited and can't wait to meet my clients to create something different and beautiful for every single one of them. I feel it's my way to change this world for the better. I love making people look better and feel good about themselves, as we all know that our look is very important. It's a message that you are sending to the world – "Here, it's me and this is who I am."

The beauty of following your dream is that when your heart is truly open to the Universe, when you want to spread only love, happiness and joy, that you want to become a better person than you were yesterday and make this world a better place to live for all of us, at that moment, somehow your dreams start to come true. Of course, like every human being, I had my down moments, my failure stories and feeling that this is it, I can't keep up. But I always say to myself, "Ok, just do something a little more today and tomorrow we will see. Just take this little extra step, just finish this little project." And little by little, step by step I am where I am now - business owner, proud hairstylist, author, TV hairstylist and makeup artist. I am telling you to always believe in yourself. It's not going to be easy, but keep going. You absolutely must love what you do if you want to succeed. It will be hard, sometimes impossible, and a normal person would quit. But if you love what you do, you start thinking outside the box and try to find different solutions to any problem or look at it from a different angle. That's what makes me keep going and taking one more step, what you will see at the end when you make it to that one extra mile.

Maybe my story will inspire somebody. If so, drop me a line on my website www.confessionsofthehairstylist.com.

I am not smarter than you. I am not better than anybody else. I am like everyone else. I just want to show that anything is possible. If I made it happen in a different country with a different language, different culture, customs, people and traditions, what is stopping you?

I am not religious, but I am spiritual. I believe that what you are spreading around the world is what you will get in return. Be grateful and don't expect joyful people to be around if you are a drama queen. Want a simple solution? Take responsibility and be in charge of your own emotions, feelings, reactions to situations and life in general. The teacher in me is sneaking out.

My main point for this chapter is to believe what your heart tells you, not what others say.

About the Author

- Certified Hair Stylist with European and Canadian experience
- Finalist of the Contessa 2013 - The Canadian Hairstylist of the Year Awards
- Leading Stylist at fashion shows and photo shoots
- TV hairstylist and makeup artist
- Trained by World Class Marvel Beauty School, Vidal Sassoon School (Canada), Euronatorals Hair Extensions Certification (Canada), Vitality's Colour School (Italy), European Hairstyle School (Ukraine)

Anastasia was born in Ukraine, Europe, into a creative family. Her grandfather Kostya was a painter; Grandmother Galina sewed the cloth; Grandmother Elena did embroidery, her father is a music teacher and musician, her mother was a teacher of languages and a writer, and her sister is a singer and a director on TV.

Anastasia also finished arts school where she studied music, sculpture, and painting, as well as where she learned the classic laws of colour, balance, proportion.

The Stylist/Colourist

A professional stylist/colourist is fundamentally different from the classic hairdresser. The name of the profession comes from the word "colour", because the colourist specializes in hair colouring. Moreover, the procedure of dying with a colourist has an independent title "colouring" to emphasize the difference from the classical multi-tone hair colouring. The stylist/colourist selects not one colour, but the range of matching colours, taking into account not only the wishes of the client, but also the colour of their eyes and skin.

There are many important things in the stylist/colourist profession: knowledge of chemistry, physics, and understanding of colour, knowledge of rules and laws in this area and, of course, experience. Colourists can combine colour with highlights, which results in different effects: from unique fancy contrasts to new-fashioned naturally looking sun-bleached hair. Well-chosen colours can even simulate the volume or emphasize the contours of a haircut.

In this area, the hairstylist has accumulated extensive experience in colouring. My hands are working for you! I am trusted by models preparing for fashion shows, business woman and Toronto fashionistas who prefer individually selected deep-coloured hair.

The stylists/colourists perform all the techniques of colouring and will correct the mistakes of other hairdressers. I will tint your hair according to all the rules of colouring, which are not always considered even by professional hairdressers, who can masterfully perform haircuts, but do not work as precisely with colouring as colourists do. The stylist/colourist designs your individual recipe of hair colouring, picking up the equipment according to your hair type and the previous history of colouring. The specialist selects the appropriate care and style just for your hair type.

www.anastasiahairdesign.com
fb: https://www.facebook.com/anastasia.kravtsova.1
fb: https://www.facebook.com/Anastasia.Metro.Hair.Designs

Testimonials

"I came to Anastasia after leaving my stylist of 10 years. I am the kind of person who avoids haircuts like the plague, dreads appointments for weeks before, and generally cries after getting it cut for a few days. Then, I met Anastasia.

From the moment I sat down in her chair, it was clear that this woman was no ordinary stylist. I was absolutely blown away by her depth of knowledge and understanding. She won my confidence and trust instantly. It was absolutely well deserved. I walked away with my hair looking the best it ever has. What's more, I walked away with the knowledge of how to take the best possible care of my hair. Anastasia does not just understand hair. She IS hair. She becomes one with the hair. She is, The Hair Whisperer.

From a beautiful boutique style salon that reflects her incredible sense of style, the top notch products and colour she uses, to her wit, charm and warmth, it truly is the best salon experience I have ever had. She goes above and beyond anything I could have expected. Anastasia has won my loyalty as a client for life."

Kelly S (Toronto)

"Honestly, it's not easy to please me, but Anastasia has not only done it – she really surprised me with the level of her skills. Trust her and you'll not be disappointed. Finally, I found a master I want to come back to!"

Julia M (Toronto)

"I had just left an appointment nearby and decided to check out Anastasia's salon. She was very welcoming and spent the time to give me a tour of her salon and chatted about the products she used and sold. I was impressed by the line; as gentle natural products are very important to me. I booked my appointment for the next day. She did a colour and cut which I love. She also listened to what my needs were and I was able to style it easily on my own. I usually don't like styling products in my hair when I leave a salon as they can be sticky and overpowering in smell. After my visit to her, my hair smelled delicious for the rest of the day and soft to the touch. The salon is adorable and cozy, and I loved the music that was playing that day. Tia, her junior stylist was very pleasant and easy to talk too. Oh, and Anastasia promised I would love her coffee and I did! Looking forward to my next cut and colour."

Nancy L (Toronto)

"I want to give a big shout out to Anastasia Metro Hair Designs (Queen and Woodbine). She is a new stylist to the 'hood and I'm so glad I booked an appointment. She was gracious and kind. Not having a chance to even eat one day, (it was one of those days) she served up a cheese, veggies and fruit plate - cappuccinos were available on the side. She took the time to truly consult and understand who I was and my lifestyle. She offered her suggestions on my colour and cut with all my "likes" in mind. If you want to be spoiled and be made to feel like a Princess, it's worth a trip to support this awesome local business."

Denise A. The Beach(es) (Toronto)

"I think that Anastasia Metro Hair Designs is the best hair salon in Toronto!! I had so many bad experiences with hairstylists (brassy colours, fried highlights and awful cuts). Anastasia does the best colour in Toronto, she knows her formulas perfectly. After my visits, I always look great and am happy and my hair is healthy. I've heard some people call her a "Blonde's Best Friend". Also, she has a great variety of different treatments. Love them!! (I'm blond, so I will try anything available). I have to mention her highlights!!! Best highlights in Toronto!!!!!!!!! Mine look so natural.... like sun-kissed streaks, never wild zebra-like. Love it!!!! I have to say that she is one of the few hairstylists who understands the difference between 0.5 inch and 5 inches, when I'm asking for a trim. So many times before her, I had bad experiences (when I asked for a trim and got half of my hair chopped). I've been with her for 2 years, and cannot thank her enough for my great-long-blond-healthy hair!! Try and you will be addicted!!!!!!!!"

Lidia K. Vaughan ON

"I am always hesitant to try new salons. I had bad experience with my high lights in the past. My hair had a lot of breakage from the lightener and the shade of high lights was yellowish, so my friend recommended Anastasia to me. I must admit, she is a Queen of the highlights. First of all, she spent a lot of time on consultation, something I had never experienced before. She advised me what colour would be the best for my skin and my style. The end result was fabulous. I love my shiny, silky hair, and this is what I have been wanting for a really long time. A new look, a hair transformation, just love it. So easy to manage. Thank you, Anastasia, you made me look and feel great."

Helen H. Toronto

"As a makeup artist, I have had the pleasure of being a client, as well as a business partner with Anastasia. We have worked together on publications and weddings, and I cannot imagine recommending anybody else to my friends and clients for anything to do with hairstyling. She's a professional, and she is a pleasure to be around; and her work speaks for itself!"

Helena L Toronto

"I am so thrilled to have finally discovered a salon that truly cares and listens to my needs. Being an Interior Designer my image is very important to my profession. My thick and wavy hair is not always manageable, but Anastasia knows just how to cut it to make it look great every time. Her salon environment is not only beautiful but comfortable and relaxing. Since my busy schedule limits my availability, I appreciate that she makes the effort to accommodate me on a moment's notice."

Zora S. (Toronto)

"I went to Anastasia after reading reviews online, and she definitely exceeded my expectations. It was one of the best haircuts I've ever had. I had in mind a different look, which Anastasia felt would require quite a bit of maintenance and after discussing my lifestyle and how I like to manage my hair, she suggested an alternate cut. She took the time to provide me with the best cut and blow dry finish and didn't rush through it. I was pleasantly surprised with the outcome and true to her word, I found that I was able to easily maintain it."

Karin K. Toronto

Bibliography

Paula's Choice. "Salon Etiquette: The Do's and Dont's of the Hairstylist/Client Relationship". Facebook. August 2, 2013. [July 12, 2016. https://www.facebook.com/notes/paulas-choice/salon-etiquette-the-dos-donts-of-the-hairstylistclient-relationship/10151743 833914004?pnref=story]

Donna Star, Writer, June 15, 2015 (internet article) https://www.quora.com/How-does-fashion-affect-our-lives-and-our-society

www.ingramcontent.com/pod-product-compliance
Lightning Source LLC
Chambersburg PA
CBHW061747270326
41928CB00011B/2401